My Big Mouth and The Ugly Truth
Taking the Stress out of Opinions VS. Facts

ISBN: 978-0-578-57869-9

DEDICATION

To Lois, you have always put a lot on hold to support my dreams

Table of Contents

ACKNOWLEDGMENTS

First and foremost, I would like to express my sincere gratitude to Dr. Christopher Thompson, general station manager at WCRN radio. His support, guidance and knowledge have been extremely valuable to me in my 10-year radio career.

This book was developed out of a series of radio interviews and without my guests this book wouldn't be possible. You trusted me with my questions and I am grateful to each and every one of you.

Thank you to my long time broadcast producers Ted A. and Shane. You're both a big part of my show and its commercial success.

Thank you, my audience for listening and being part of the show.

1

DR. GERARD LAMEIRO

Gary: We are joined by Dr. Gerard Lameiro. Dr. Lameiro is a political analyst and expert on forecast models. He's the author of five books. More Great News for America, which I believe is coming out very soon. Great News for America, Renewing America and Its Heritage of Freedom, Choosing the Good Life, and America's Economic War. Good afternoon, doctor.

Dr. Lameiro: Hi. It's great to be with you.

Gary: It's great to have you. Where are you? Are you in sunny California, or where are you?

Dr. Lameiro: I am in sunny Colorado.

Gary: Colorado. That's all right. I love Colorado. That's great. That's a good place to be, Colorado. There's a lot of stuff I want to try and talk with you about today in this half hour. Let's start with the last night's State of the Union address. All in all, how do you think the president fared last night?

Dr. Lameiro: Well, he did quite well. In the YouGov poll, 75% of listeners liked it. And in some other polls, we see that 43% of democrats liked it. I think that's probably worrying the democrats in a major way because when you have your own party liking the opposition parties' president, that's not a good signal for them for the fall.

Gary: No.

Dr. Lameiro: So I think he did a good job. He used the word we 104 times. He used other words like that that were unifying words quite a few times. And I think basically he was trying to reach out. But there's no doubt he has a conservative message. And for those liberals in the audience, the Democrats, they were not happy because they didn't like his policy.

Gary: Yeah, I know. They don't like his demeanor it's amazing. You sit, you watch the speech, and you watch the Democrats, and they're sitting there. Okay, they don't want to get up and clap. They don't want to clap. But what kills me, and I used to say this even when Barack Obama was president, and some of the Republicans, you can't sit there with at least a smile on your face. It's just amazing. They look like they were in so much pain. And I'm saying to myself, "You're in pain because you're just as responsible for where we are today as anybody else whether it's the economy, immigration, North Korea." I mean, it's just an amazing thing when you watch that. Though it's all optics.

Dr. Lameiro: The thing that amazed me most, actually, of all the different responses that in the chamber were the Black Caucus. I mean, the black Americans, when he mentioned the fact that the black unemployment was the lowest it's ever been in recorded history of that statistic, I would think they would have been smiling, clapping, and thinking that they're compatriots there. Black Americans had done better, but they weren't happy at all to hear that good news.

Gary: Yeah. I was quite surprised. I mean, look, you may not get up, and cheer, or clap on other policy matters, but when that specific item came up and specifically the stat on it, I would've thought they would've been happy to hear that, which I know I was and a lot of other American. Because it's whether you vote for a candidate or not, and this is my own feeling, you still want the country to succeed. I mean, it's in the best of both interests. And I think that's probably the problem, doctor, now. We're at this stalemate where it's like this alignment. I'm not going to cross it for your guy, and you're not going to cross it for mine. That's probably why we're in the position we're in.

Dr. Lameiro: Yeah. Well, there's no doubt there's ideological barrier there. In fact, I wrote a book in 2010, which you mentioned earlier, America's Economic War. And really it was the war, the political war, over economics. I called America's Economic War, and it was sort of the fight between those that really loves socialism, big government, high taxes. They think that's the right answer and those who believe in free enterprise, freedom. They want the government out of their business. They like low regulations.

Dr. Lameiro: Well, there's a warfare between those two philosophies, those two ideologies. And that there still today. I mean, I wrote about that in 2010 when the book came out, and we're still fighting that same war, so to speak, because those people just don't like a conservative approach to government.

Gary: Right. Right. And there's nothing that will change their minds. I thought the president did a great job with the guests that he had in the audience. The family, the two families that lost their daughter to the gang members, and the parents whose son came back from North Korea there and passed away. That was heart-wrenching. And just everyone in general: The young boy, the soldier, the ice agent, the police officers, the fireman in California. I think he did a great job of the way he brought them into the conversation and out of the conversation. But I wasn't surprised. I mean, that's Donald Trump. He's a showman. And I think that worked out well. He talked about the economy. He talked about immigration, North Korea. Immigration, I just can't see how we're going to allow nothing to happen on immigration.

Dr. Lameiro: Oh, I think something's going to happen. I think there's going to be the elimination of the lottery visa. I think we're going to have elimination. Actually, it's a widow going down of the immigration. Just strictly nuclear family, parents and children, basically. Not everybody in your brother: uncles, aunts, 14th cousins, all that. Everything. I think those are going by the wayside. The real issue is, what do you do about the dreamers, the DACA folks? I think that's yet to be determined.

Gary: Yeah. If you read or listen to the Democrats, or Chuck Schumer, no wall. There's no way we're giving into the wall. I don't think Trump, President Trump, can move forward without getting something, getting the wall or some sort of wall.

Dr. Lameiro: Well, I think he's going to get the wall. That's a matter of timing. Is it going to happen now? Is it going to happen before the election, the electoral, and the congressional elections? Or is it going to happen 2019? I think it's going to be determined largely by how the Democrats do in the polling. Because if they continue the buck now from and buck his agenda, they are also bucking the American people.

Gary: Right. Right. I think the American people will, at that point, be just totally frustrated, and the results of the election at that point may speak for themselves.

Dr. Lameiro: Well, I think what's he's going to do is if they think that they have to go along with some of Donald Trump's agenda in order to get elected, they'll do it. Otherwise, they're going to wind up losing their office, and we're going to have a much more conservative congress in 2019.

Gary: And as far as North Korea, I think it was that young gentleman that was there from North Korea. I'm hoping that the quiet conversation about North Korea now it's not necessarily beating the news down every night, but something's going on in the back room. But sooner or later, doctor, that has to be addressed. Look what happened in Hawaii, though. We're finding out that one individual panic with the threat of missiles coming in. But there is the risk of this happening. Look, I would not want to be the president or anyone in his cabinet having that worry over my head every night.

Dr. Lameiro: Well, I'll tell you, it is the most important thing the president could is to protect the nation. Right now it appears like they have made plans to bomb, bomb. I'm talking about the North Korean. They have plans on the board to attack San Diego, which is a big military base where our navy stations. A lot of our navy is there. And they have the capability of hitting virtually every major American city. Now, the question is, do they have the nuclear technology to sit on top of those ICBMs as they now have?

Dr. Lameiro: It appears that they either have it or close to having it. But I think the big thing is, not so much that they have all of that, but they're belligerent. I mean, they continue to threaten attacking the US. I mean, that's what's really dangerous. If you put the weapons in people's hands who want to use it, that is incredibly dangerous. Or if they want to threaten us and say, "You do this, or you do that, or give us South Korea or we're going to bomb you." I mean, who knows what kind of threats and blackmail they could use against that.

I think we're ready to attack if we need to. I think there may be more type attacks where we knocked out their nuclear capabilities. I think there are more attacks being planned to knock out their ICBM. In other words, it's not a full-scale war, but small attack, but we're also prepared for something really major. For example, if they shoot a missile at the B1 bombers in Guam, and that, or they do something else like go and attack South Korea. So, there are a lot of possibilities. I think we're prepared for them. I think Trump is tough enough to do something. I do not think he'd allow San Diego to be knocked offline, and have no attack back. I think there's some on the left who would allow that to happen.

Gary: Right? I agree with you.

Dr. Lameiro: But negotiated through San Diego. I don't think he'll allow that to happen.

Gary: No. No. We have the Olympics coming up, which I'm hoping he's going to be on his best behavior. They've agreed to him bringing some athletes, quote-unquote, athletes there and whomever else. So we would hope that that would not be something where he would try. You've got the world's spotlight on you at that point. So hopefully, he would not do anything at that point.

Dr. Lameiro: Well, I'll tell you, I think he's trying to buy time. He is being squeeze up financially by some of the countries of the world. Not 100%. All the different sanctions placed on his country by the UN have not been followed exactly the way they should. But generally speaking, he's heard it. He's also, if you follow him closely, find out that he's killing a lot of his military leaders. He's getting rid of them. He's executing them, because he's worried that they're going to overthrow him. That's going on as we speak. But the biggest thing is, Donald Trump has military reaction. He's got three aircraft carriers that's been sitting off his coast, plus the nuclear triad submarine. That is an enormous amount of power. In fact, it's been about, oh, I think 11 years, give or take, since three aircraft carrier task forces were in the same spot at the same time in the world. That's an enormous firepower. We can basically turn North Korea into a power thing.

Gary: Hopefully, it won't come to that. No, I agree with-

Dr. Lameiro: That's right.

Gary: I agree with you 100%. We're speaking with Dr. Gerard Lameiro. Well, you're listening to Business, Politics, and Lifestyles. My name is Gary. We're going to take a break and we'll come back. I want to talk to the doctor about the FISA memo.

Gary: We're speaking with Dr. Gerard Lameiro, who's a political analyst and author. Occupying the news the last week or so and picking up momentum every day are these a FISA memos, and will they be released? It sounds like the president is going to release it. It's amazing talking to people. They don't even really understand what FISA really is. They're making assumptions of what they think it is, or what maybe they want it to be to protect their side, but they don't really get it and don't really understand what it is and what you're allowed to do with it.

Dr. Lameiro: Right. Well, FISA, F-I-S-A, pronounced FISA is the Foreign Intelligence Surveillance Act of 1978 it was initiated by Senator Ted Kennedy from Massachusetts back then. It was signed into law by a President Jimmy Carter at the time. And basically, it was an offshoot of Watergate, believe it or not, when apparently Nixon was accused of or did, depending on what specific allegation it was, did spying on American soil. In other words, behind that you usually think of like spying on the Russians, having a covert operative by the CIA or something like that in another country.

Dr. Lameiro: At that time, apparently, Nixon did some spying on American, and that was a concern because The Fourth Amendment against the illegal search and seizure. And so, they created this act. And basically, it dealt with allowing

Americans to spy on foreign powers that were operating within the US, maybe talking to somebody in the US. The issue was, how do you protect The Fourth Amendment rights of Americans?

Dr. Lameiro: And they said, "Well, you have to go to a FISA court, and get a FISA warrant that allows you for national security reasons to spy on these foreign individuals that may be talking to Americans to find out if something funny was going on." So that's kind of the history of it. But apparently, the controversy now is that the Democratic Party, the Obama administration and high ranking officials and DOG and DOJ. I'm sorry. Department of Justice and FBI, might have illegally obtained FISA warrant to spy on the Trump campaign in order to, somehow, help a Hillary Clinton get elected.

Dr. Lameiro: That, in itself, is a scandal and a violation of the law. And by the way, I believe, and I'm not a lawyer. I'm an analyst. But I believe my understanding of FISA law is that anytime you violate it, you get a $10,000 fine, and up to five years of jail. So that's a real crime we're talking about if you lie to a judge to get a warrant to spy on foreigners and Americans in the US. So you can't just take it lightly.

Dr. Lameiro: And it appears like this is the real controversy. It appears like the Trump dossier, which was paid for by the Clinton administration to dig up dirt on presidential candidate Trump, and paid for by the Clinton campaign and the DNC that that particular dossier was used by the FBI to seek out, get a FISA warrant so they could go spy on the Trump campaign. And that, in and of itself, is almost banana republic for trying to get involved in a presidential campaign using, if you will, fake information.

Gary: So, I'd have to assume that if this memo gets released, and if you believe what you heard last night, the president, when someone asked him that question, said, "Definitely, it's going to be released." You think the American people will be in shock with what they read I mean, sometimes I wonder what it takes to shock the American people. But do you think they'll be in shock what they'll read in this memo, or?

Dr. Lameiro: I think anybody's objective is going to be in shock. Apparently, this memo, four-page memo written by the House Intelligence Committee, so people with the capability of getting secret information. Apparently, it's going to basically show that there was interference in the presidential election, but it wasn't Russian collusion. It was Clinton campaign collusion, and maybe Obama administration collusion to support Donald Trump's election. And that is going to shock a lot of people. My guess is the Democrats, many of them, will say, "I don't believe it. It can't be true. Must be fake."

Gary: Right. Right. Yeah, they'll be reversing the fake news issue.

Dr. Lameiro: Right. So the question is, who's got the real evidence? I think that all of this four-page memo is backed up with all sorts of documents, and evidence. What the Republicans are calling for is all the backup information get released as well. And that will be the next call. Once this comes out, I think they're going to say, "Let's let out all the rest of the information." And I think in a democracy, we need to see all the information. I'm in favor of that. The Democrats part of the controversy is the Democrats want to release their own memo, which apparently is not fake based with any particular information, but just basically accuses the Republicans of issuing a fake memo. I mean, this is a he said she said kind of thing.

Dr. Lameiro: But ultimately, you got to look at the evidence. I think the American people when they see the evidence and find out. I'm speculating too because I haven't seen the evidence, but I'm speculating based on the kinds of things a lot of people have said in congress that this is shocking to see that something like this could happen. That a system, which is designed to keep Americans free not to do illegal searches and seizures of people was actually afforded. Much in the same way, by the way, I might say is the IRS. The IRS, I think, there's clear evidence now. The IRS would not be a Tea Party group, a nonprofits status-

Gary: That is right.

Dr. Lameiro: Because they didn't want the Tea Party groups to have the chance to campaign against Barrack Obama in 2012. I think in the same way that the IRS was politicized, and that, and weaponized against the enemies of that administration, I think they're seeing the same thing here. The SBI highest levels, not the rank and file, the good agents that worked every day, but the high-level executive appointees, and that a political appointees made into a political organization.

Gary: And how high do you think this will go as far as ex-President Obama, or Hillary Clinton? I mean, do you think it will reach that point where they're not, maybe, sleeping as well at night?

Dr. Lameiro: I doubt if they are sleeping as well, or they may think they're going to skate on this because they've skated on so many other things. But I think the answer to this is with regard to Hillary Clinton, I think she will face justice. I think they all will. Because this is just the tip of the iceberg with the Clinton, because this is one thing that went funny. But for example, it looks like the FEC laws, the Federal Election laws, were violated. Because when you spend $9 million to create a smear dossier on Trump, that's actually a campaign expense that has to be reported. You can't just spend $9 million.

Dr. Lameiro: But what they did was they gave five million of that to Perkins Coy, a law firm, as a kind of a breakout so that it looks like it was legal fees, but it's actually something totally different. And that would in itself maybe violate the laws. But there are other laws too. For example, taking over the DNC, which Donna Brazil said in her book that Hillary Clinton took over the DNC while there was a primary in progress, which is a problem because you're using DNC resources for her campaign. She basically kept Bernie Sanders from getting the nomination. I mean, Bernie Sanders, his supporters ought to be ready to go to court themselves, and maybe in some cases they have or will. There are so many issues. The pay for play, when Hillary Clinton was secretary of state. The disappearance of all of her State Department emails, not just her emails on private servers, but also the other email that they apparently went to class, her records went with her, and those are government records.

Dr. Lameiro: There are so many questionable things and potential crimes. I think she's going to face criminal charges. I think some of the top people at the FBI are also in deep trouble, and also at the DOJ as well. Or, for example, meeting with Chris Steele, the spy, meeting with Fusion GPS, a political opposition research firm, without telling that the Department of Justice is a problem. That's why he got demoted. His wife working for and being paid to write the Trump dossier. That's a problem. There a lot of people who're going to face a different types of charges, I think.

Gary: Yeah, and it's sad. What upsets me is there's many good people than DOJ and the FBI. Just you know how this stuff works. Everyone gets that it's all tainted. They all look bad for the time being when it's probably just hopefully just a few at the top. But if this is the case, and this starts to unravel, at some point, I think, you really have to look into the FBI, the DOJ, and make sure things are operating as they should because it becomes dangerous for the country assault. Doctor, we're at the bottom of the hour. How can people find you and get ahold of you?

Dr. Lameiro: Greatnewsforamerica.com is my website and 2016 book in which I made 10 predictions for the 2016 election. Nine of them came out true. Some people say I got all 10 true. By the way, I also predicted Donald Trump months before he got elected. My prediction came out almost exactly right.

Gary: Yeah, I know. I follow you through your website, and which you have a great website, by the way.

Dr. Lameiro: Thank you.

Gary: A lot of great information. Yeah, you are the predictive. There's no doubt about it. You had some great prediction there. It was great speaking with you, and I hope to have you back sometime, and we'll continue with the conversation.

Dr. Lameiro: My new book, by the way, is coming out in a few weeks, More Great News for America. That'll be out. That's got some eight new predictions.

Gary: We'll have to get ahold of it, and I'll read it, and then call you back as they start falling into place.

Dr. Lameiro: All right. Well, thanks.

Gary: Thank you, doctor.

2

ANTHONY SCARAMUCCI

Gary: We are now joined on the line with Anthony Scaramucci author of " Trump, The Blue-Collar President". Good morning and welcome to the show.

Anthony: Hey Gary, good morning.

Gary: How are you?

Anthony: You know I'm doing great, I'm out here in L.A. I did Bill Maher show last night with Stormy Daniels, obviously I'll tell you a little bit about that, but I watched that game to its conclusion and I'm going over to Dodger Stadium tonight and since I'm a Mets fan and I'm also Italian, the enemy of my enemy is my friend, I'll be rooting for you guys tonight.

Gary: I hear you.

Anthony: You can't be in love with the Yankees if you're a Mets fan in New York.

Gary: No, I know that and I think the Red Sox will prevail over time here. They got a great team.

Anthony: Yeah, it's amazing. They play like a machine, I mean, that game was amazing last night, but their entire season has been machine like in terms of what they do on the ball field, unbelievable. So, I still got the Red Sox in five. I said that before the series started. Let's see what happens.

Gary: Well you know not only are we getting to speak to you about your book, we got a first-hand account of the ball game, which is even better. That's great. So Anthony, I got to ask you a few questions. First of all, how did you become friends with Donald Trump? First of all, the book is incredible. I love your book it's incredible.

Anthony: Oh, I appreciate it.

Gary: I want to hear it from you, how you and Donald Trump became friends.

Anthony: Well, I really did try to write an honest book. Which put a lot of my work in there, a lot of the mistakes that I made, things that I wish I had done differently. But it's also a tale about how you have to pick yourself up when you are making those kinds of mistakes, otherwise you can't go forward. All good entrepreneurs know that they're gonna take a lot of risk in their life and so you can't have a no stoner regret on your neck as you're going forward in life. I try to point that out in the book. But my friendship started with him in the mid 90s. I wouldn't say friendship as much as an awestruck acquaintanceship. I was in my early 30s. He was the very famous guy my boss at Goldman Sachs knew and introduced us.

And I wouldn't say we had a super closeness or anything like that but over the years we saw each other at big social events in New York, charity events, sporting events and so forth. It wasn't until the 2012 Mitt Romney campaign that we really started to develop a closer relationship. We had worked on several fundraising events for the Governor, Governor Romney. We did a call-a-thon with Mr. Trump. I'll tell you what, he was very effective with these robocalls during the primaries for Mitt Romney. We did a ton of those with him and he was always, always popular with those blue-collar people and I really do try to explain why. But it really wasn't until after The Apprentice was over, he called me a few weeks before The Apprentice finale and asked to have breakfast with him. So the morning after that Apprentice finale, he looked at me straight on, in his office, dead serious, " I'm running for president.". I basically laughed at him as I recant in the book. I'm like, "You're not doing it, it's a publicity stunt." And I was wrong obviously and he was very, very right.

And then I also talk about our first fundraising meeting after I had left the Bush campaign when Jeb had withdrawn from the race and I actually brought one of your old senators with me who was a friend of mine, Senator Scott Brown. So Scott Brown and I went to his office on the 26th floor of the Trump Tower and started to lay out what we thought were the fundraising mechanisms that he would need to power up the campaign post Republican Party Convention and the nominations.

Gary:

There was a part though that you and him, you played like a political antagonist, where you challenged Donald Trump, when was that?

Anthony:

Yeah no question, and I looked at that part of the story too because it tells you a lot about his personality. So I was on Maria Bartiromo's show on the Fox Business Network and the President or then the candidate, was on Fox and Friends just wailing on the hedge fund industry so I was like, "Hey man, don't pick on my industry." And so I started up with him and then there was the funniest thing in the book where he's actually calling me a couple hours after we were hitting each other and he said, "Hey, come up to my office." I went up there and he said, " Why are you being so rough on me?" I said, " What are you talking about? You're hitting the hedge fund industry." And then he looked over at me in the typical

New Yorker way, where he's like you know what I actually started this fight. You're not the one that started it. And then I looked at him and said'" You always say the hedge fund guys don't pay any taxes, I'm paying 53% marginal tax rate. And then Trump looks over at me and goes, " Well, you know let me tell you something. Let me introduce you to a new accountant. Your accountant stinks."

And then we had a big laugh about that. So, he was never really sore about that. In fact, on the Saturday after I started. I did my press conference on a Friday, the 21st of July. But on that Saturday, he sent out a Tweet saying, " Hey, you can't blame Anthony Scaramucci. I'm sorta the one that started that fracas back in the campaign." So he was always good with that. I never had a real. But I know the media liked playing that up. Oh look at this guy that was super sour on Trump. Now he's a Trump sycophant.

You guys get to know me or we spend more time on the phone together, you'll find I'm really not as thick-skinned. I'll tell the guy, and unfortunately most people, exactly what I think. And I always tell people that work for me sycophancy is not loyalty. In fact, if anything it's selfishness and self-preservation. The real loyal people are the ones that are able to be honest and are able to be constructive and helpful to somebody. So, I've always to be in that category with President Trump.

Gary:	We're speaking with Anthony Scaramucci, author of Trump, The Blue Collar President. You know, a lot of rich guys try to run for president and just couldn't connect with the American people. Donald Trump does haven an incredible connection with the average guy; you'd call him the blue-collar worker Where does that come from?

Anthony:

It's a great question because I did a ton of research on this for the book. I had gone back into those areas. You remember my hometown is only about six, seven miles from where the president grew up. And I interviewed some families that lived in the Trump apartment building that Fred Trump had built. And I interviewed people that knew the president when he was in his early to mid-twenties and I tell some great stories in the book about him collecting coins at a vending machine at his father's apartment complex or from the laundry facilities at his dad's apartment. And I talk about one scene, it's actually a family that the Scaramucci's are very close to Caruana family where they can't make the rent and Fred Trump is standing at the doorway with a very tall Donald J Trump. And it's in the mid-seventies and the patriarch, Fred, turns to this blue-collar worker and says," You know, you've been a very honorable guy. You've paid your rent on time. I know you're gonna find another job. Why don't we wait a month Lets revisit this in a month. I'm here to help you out."

It's not a story you often hear about the Trump family. But I think it's very revelatory in terms of the formation of the president's relationship with blue-collar people. He was on those construction sites. He worked with them. He interacted with them. I think this is a neat part of his characteristic, whether you like him or dislike him, he was able to win the hearts and minds of so many people from these blue-collar neighborhoods. By the way, you guys probably know this, and I do support it with statistics. But, 60% of the people below the median income line that actually voted in the 2016 election, voted for the president. It was the coast and people that had higher income, the probably voted more for Secretary Clinton than what is now President Trump.

Gary:

Yeah I mean there's no doubt that he understands where the core of America is. You know, the fiber of America. The middle class. When he came to Massachusetts, to Worcester, when he first started running and I was covering him at that night and saw the different people there. And the way he talked and the way people just gravitated toward him. It was incredible, Anthony. You could tell right away that this guy had IT. You know that this is what America Was looking for, at least at this point in time.

<table><tr><td>Anthony:</td><td>Not only do I agree with that, I also point out that, Democrats get upset with me, but I think, if you're a Democrat, read the book. Understand how he stole your base. What he did was, Democrats were focused on things, not saying they're bad things, but they were focused on things like social issues, the environment, the sanitizing of people's voices when they talked to each other, he notion of political correctness. And while they were doing all that, they were effectively ignoring policies that were necessary for middle and lower middle class people to do better with their lives and to try to raise their living standards. And so they took that core bread and butter constituency for granted. It's probably been three decades of them doing that. And that created this vacuum that the president was able to exploit. So, in many ways, what he did is a political, it's almost like a, I don't know how to describe it, an anomaly.</td></tr></table>

He hijacked the Republican Party. Took it from the establishment who didn't want him to have the nomination. And then he reached over and grabbed the bait from the Democratic Party and moved it to his ledger. So, I write about it in the book. I write about how he was able to do that. But then I also write about his family. So you can see the arc of his family's success I juxtapose it where my family had a different American story but it was still a classic, striving American Dream sorta story. Where my folks were like, "You're gonna do your homework or you're gonna get hit with a belt." I'm sure you guys had the same experience growing up as we did. And my dad was a tough construction worker. He didn't take any guff in the house. But he always thought that his kids, if they had followed the rules of law, gone to great schools. I went to two great Boston schools Tufts and Harvard Law School so that we would have a chance to do well.

When I point it out in the book, my pops had a great middle class wage. Forty-two years with the same construction company. But unfortunately, those wages today are down telling us, about 32 and a half percent in real economic terms. That's form the forces of globalization, form the forces of robotics and excess automation. So those families that were aspirational in the sixties, seventies and eighties, have become somewhat desperate today because they really can't capture that middle class experience. Again, whether people like it or not, the president did see that and he was certainly somebody that those people gravitated to and he still has a lot of strong support in those areas.

Gary: As you point out in the book, here's a guy that used a shovel, understands how a building is built. Really understands electrical systems, the whole engineering process. But, to me, has he built that Trump brand? I don't think Donald Trump really changed. He didn't become. You think of a billionaire as a snoot that most very wealthy rich people don't wanna talk to blue collar people. Let's call it the way it is, Anthony. But he's not that guy.

Anthony: He's not that guy and, let me tell you something, in that genre of that super wealthy circle, you know, I can't speak to that cultural society, if you will, in Boston, but I can tell you, in New York, it's somewhat clannish.

Gary: Yup.

Anthony:

And so they never allowed him into the reindeer games right? No. He was sort of Rudolph the red-nosed billionaire. They left him out of the reindeer games. I think, in a weird way, that brought him way closer to the middle class and to the people that I describe in my book. I am on the opposite and I do write this in the book very honestly, I got sucked into that. I was at Goldman Sachs. I hung out in the salons of the wealthy. I went to the World Economic Forum and gave speeches there. And I started to get the confirmed biases and the concentric circles of the wealthy. And I'm not embarrassed to admit this to you guys and I certainly wrote it in the book. I didn't see the disparity that was going on in the country with the amount of magnitude that I needed to see it until I joined president Trump on the campaign. And that's my own fault, I got sucked into that system if you will. As I was trying to strive for financial independence for myself and my family.

And so would I caution my friends, our your listeners who, hopefully they have a great lifestyle and are hanging out with very rich people, pay attention to what's going on in middle America because there's an economic struggle going on there that's gonna still have great political ramifications over the next ten to twenty years. Frankly, it took a billionaire who was living adjacent to the Tiffany's jewelry store in midtown Manhattan, to show it to me and I'm trying to explain it in my book to our potential readers.

Gary:

Do you still speak with the president?

Anthony:

Last time I spoke to him was around Labor Day. I'm not one of these guys who's gonna pick up the phone and call him and then I can say to you," oh Hey I talked to the president yesterday.' If I had something to call him about that I thought was helpful to him, by all means I would certainly call him. The last time we spoke, it was really related to the

European trade situation and the NASA thing. I wanted to give him my perspective. As a money manager, I run an eleven-billion-dollar fund that I started. And I said to the president, "Look. I may not have been your best communications director but I've been running money for thirty years. And I wanted to give him a perspective on what I was seeing in the marketplace related to some of the rhetoric around trade. I think he was appreciative of the call. We had a rigorous discussion. I don't wanna be that self-important guy that goes oh yeah I just talked to the president yesterday. I'll call him if I think it's relevant to him and, obviously, he calls me. And he's the President of the United States you stand up guy. You call him back in 10 seconds.

Gary: To me the media, maybe it was CNN I saw you on, where they'll take a word that you used, you know?

Anthony: Yeah.

Gary: Headlines. Anthony Scaramucci calls Trump a liar. It's amazing and then when you listen to it, just the fluck of a word they change what you're saying Anthony.

Anthony: Yes, it's brutal. I was making the point that he has an embellisher of a story. Yes, he coughs up these stories. You gotta understand something, he's doing that, and if you wanna use the word while in its context. He is doing that because he knows you're gonna be like a hall monitor. He knows you're gonna be like a proctor.

Gary: Exactly.

Anthony: Or the Catholic nun that's gonna call him out on it. And you're gonna spend all your time in this distress and anger mode on your television shows while he's out there galvanizing his support. You'd be so much better off. I made this point on Bill Maher show last night. You'd be so much better off, yeah you wanna call him out for a liar because it hurts your moral consciousness, God bless you. But all politicians lie. Let's say he's the worst, he's the worst Pinocchio ever. Who cares? Focus on what he did. If you wanna compete with President Trump, figure out how you're gonna reform your product line and your policies related to blue-collar people.

Gary: I agree.

Anthony: If you wanna spend all your time on CNN fact checking him, he's laughing and so is his base. And that was the point I was trying to make that there was actually premeditation to his communication strategy. They wanna call it lying. I had to finally capitulate yeah, of course, it's a lie slash a mistruth but it was really trying to explain the strategy. It's more strategic than it is hey I'm just gonna get up this morning and tell a lie.

Gary: Yeah. No.

Anthony: That was the point I was making.

Gary: As soon as I heard you say it, I said to myself, " Oh here we go," because not I know the way they're gonna play that. Just a couple quick things and I know you have to go. Will the president run again in 2020?

Anthony: No question. Yeah yeah. He's already raised more money than any other presidential candidate, any other incumbent in US history. He's up to 111, 112 million dollars. I predict he'll have close to 2 billion dollars to run with when he gets there. And I also predict that he'll be a very formidable competitor. And I tell my Democratic friends, if you're gonna run against the president, you're gonna have an internationally recognized nickname for the rest of your life. Just get ready for it, Okay? And, God only knows what it will be. Governor, there's a funny scene in the book where the president says the walk around the plane. Governor Walker says, " Hey, why'd you drop out of the race so quickly?" And Walker looks over to him and says, " Hey I had to get out of the race before you nicknamed me. I didn't think I could survive it." So just be careful. You may be getting DNA tests when it's probably not the best idea to do that. You know that sorta thing. He does it to you.

Gary: Any political plans in your horizon at any point in time?

Anthony: Well, listen, I was on the verge of a divorce. I do write about it in the book. I love my wife and love my family and so, you know, I gotta be honest with ya, I probably will never go into politics because I've gotta keep those priorities in check. So let me tell you something guys, you know this. It is horrible. It is very very rough on families. And they spare nobody. So they go after your young children even and so I sorta feel like I need to shield my family from that sorta stuff. But I'm not a politician so I'm not gonna sit here and tell you oh I would never do it because, you never know. I mean you know what, I don't wanna be on a mic saying I said I never would do it and ten years later I'm doing it and someone's playing it and saying oh he said he never would do this. Typical politician. We'll have to see but my guess is no but you never know what life brings.

Gary: No. You're great. We were speaking with Anthony Scaramucci, author of Trump, the Blue-Collar President. Where can they get your book, Anthony? Just about anywhere.

Anthony: You go to Barnes and Noble, Books A million, Amazon.com. You could download it on any of your mobile phone devices or I Pad or Kindle. It's a quick read. It's 300 pages. I put a lot of stuff in there. What to do when life is giving you lemons. I have a whole lemonade recipe in that book entitled the twelfth day. And that's metaphorical for me because I spent eleven days in the White House. I get blasted out of there and I'm ripped up in the International media. And how do you handle yourself on that twelfth day? How do you pick yourself back up and get going again? I think there's something in there for everybody and I hope you guys will go out and read it and tell me what you think about it.

Gary: No, it's a great book and, when you come up here for the Red Sox victory parade, give me a call. I'll take you to dinner.

Anthony: Hey Red Sox in five. I'll be there tonight with my sons. I'm really looking forward to it. God bless you.

Gary: Anthony, thanks for taking the time this morning.

Anthony: All right. All the best.

3

JUDGE JEANINE PIRRO

Gary: Right now we are joined by Judge Jeanine Pirro. Judge Jeanine is the host of Fox News Justice with Judge Jeanine and the author of Liars, Leakers, and Liberals: The Case Against the Anti-Trump Conspiracy. Good morning, judge.

Judge Jeanine: Good morning. How are you doing?

Gary: I'm doing wonderful. I must say that I started listening to your book. I bought your book audio and the hard copy of it, and it is incredible. But before we get to that, I'm sure everyone has asked you this question, but I do want to talk to you about The View the other day because I've watched that tape over and over again, of that situation. First of all, the look on your face I think said it all. I give you a lot of credit because I don't think I would have been as calm as you would have been. But the more I listen to that, Judge, the more I feel that it seems to me it may have been orchestrated that that was part of Whoopi's plan. She was going to get out there and spew her what she calls information to her guests, to her audience, because I don't think she's capable of having a conversation to discuss facts and other ideas.

Judge Jeanine: Well, I think that the proof is in the pudding as you say. Again, if you watch the segments, and there were two segments on The View on my book, Liars, Leakers, and Liberals. I went on The View in order to talk about a book. I mean they invited me, and in the end, I and five people who were with me were literally thrown out. It wasn't pretty, but I think that what we've got to try to do is to make sure that people understand why we are as long as we are for this country, for law and order, and for the presidency. And that's why I did it. I mean people say, "Well, why would you go on that?" Well, I believe that we've got an obligation to try to convince as many people as possible, or at least give them an idea of what the other side is saying. Because it was really a microcosm of what's going on in America today where people just don't want to hear the other side.

So, I write a book. It has heavy footnotes. It's a very easy read, and by the way I appreciate you getting the audio as well as the hard copy of Liars, Leakers. But for me, it was a rather stunning experience, and I'm going to talk about it on my show tonight, Justice with Judge Jeanine on Fox News Channel at 9:00 p.m., and then I want to talk about all the stuff that's going on in the world today, and the fact that there is a hard left that is determined to overthrow the presidency and disenfranchise those of us who put Donald Trump in the oval office.

And this conspiracy started long before he even took over the oval office, and it's evident from the emails and text messages of Peter Struck and his girlfriend, Lisa Pate, where they say they're going to stop it, he's not going to get elected, they'll stop it, he's this loathsome human being. And in the end, we'll get the insurance policy in the event that the unthinkable happens, and that is when someone like Donald Trump gets elected.

Now what we're doing is we're listening to nothing more than a nonstop rustic delusion where everyone is saying, "Oh, it's there. The evidence is going to be there." But there is no evidence, because the Department of Justice and FBI decided they would stage an investigation, and the counterintelligence investigation. The whole thing is very sad.

<table>
<tr><td>Gary:</td><td>Yeah. I mean no matter what the facts are, Judge, there narrative is the same. You point out a number of things in your book, but if you lay the facts out, they still don't want to believe it. They still come to their own conclusions no matter what the facts are, which is a sad commentary of what is going on in the world today, and especially in this country, and especially when you can't even have that conversation with people.</td></tr>
<tr><td>Judge Jeanine:</td><td>Well, yeah, and that is symptomatic of the hard left, and the progressives, and the socialists, who are looking to shut down the right. Whenever somebody's going to a University campus, and they're shut down by antifa or right-hating individuals. The truth is that they say that unless you follow their thinking, their thoughts, and their way of looking at the world, you're a fascist, when in truth they're the fascists, because they're preventing us from being able to say what we're entitled to say under the first amendment. Everything is backwards, upside down, and inside out. And my book, Liars and Leakers, I track what happened in the last election, but I also talk about the man, Donald Trump, who I've known for almost three decades, and the fact that this is someone who hasn't changed one bit in all the years that I've known him, that forever he was pulled in and sought out for interviews and print media, television, movies, and then all of a sudden he says I'm going to run for president as a Republican, nothing changed with him, but then he was seen as the Devil Incarnate. And this is something that we in America try to prevent when we elected Donald Trump, because we didn't like the way the country was going when Barack Obama was there.

Now, that they hissy fitted the left is growing into this kind of shut them down, shut them up, and let's impeach, over through, or now charge Donald Trump with treason. I don't think anyone alive has ever seen anything like this before.</td></tr>
</table>

Gary:	No, you can't make it up, and on a daily basis it changes. But anyone connected to the president is fair game. If someone in his family wears an odd color pair of shoes, that's an issue. Supporters and voters are marked. And it's just anyone associated with this president, it's crazy. Your fair game. And that could be voters, like myself or yourself. Your fair game if you support Donald Trump.
Judge Jeanine:	Well, I think we've seen it over and over with people like Maxine Waters, saying if you see him, make a crowd, shut him down, or whatever it is that she said. And with Sarah Sanders and her family were forced out of a restaurant after Kirstjen Nielson, homeland security, a cabinet member was asked to leave a restaurant. When Pam Bondi, the Attorney General, and isn't that interesting, all conservative women. When Pam Bondi goes to a movie, they create a crowd to force her out. I've never seen the right do anything like this.

There's always been a left and a right, and people on both sides are very dug in, but I've never seen it like this. And that's why I wrote the book. And in the book, I also talk about the Republicans in name only, who would rather join the Democrats against the newly elected then they would in supporting their president. And we see it time and time again. I've said before that if you're at the tip of the spear, you are the beginning of the change, of dramatic change, if anything, you're going to suffer push back, and every day this president has incoming. But he gets up and accomplishes an economy better than it's been in decades. African Americans, minority unemployment never lower, more jobs than there are people to fill them. It's sad what they're doing. America needs to understand that in 2018, this election is going to be every bit as important as 2016.

Gary:	And I agree with you. As far as the president, and he does take incoming on a daily basis, and the left will ignore all of

the accomplishments on the jobs that market the economy, but how do you survive, Judge, this type of incoming on a daily basis? I mean, over time, it has to wear. I know Donald Trump is one tough guy, but it has to wear on you.

Judge Jeanine: Well, clearly, but I know Donald Trump. I've known him, as I say in the book, and I talk about what he is like as a man. He's a force of nature. Donald Trump has just incredible instincts, so when he decided to take on the press, everyone said that was suicide, that you don't take on the press. Well, he took on the press, and he won. And Americans instinctively understood, although they did know for sure that something was off, and that's why they elected the outsider. And this outsider is someone who is accustomed to going into a den of lions and coming out unscathed. That's the man. That's who he is. And I've spoken with him personally many, many, many times, and he said to me, "You know Jeanine, my family didn't sign up for this. I did."

And he is clear that he is ready for the fight and not just ready for it, he's producing. I mean America has never been as great as shape and quickest turnaround as they have been with this business man outsider president. And Liars, Leakers, and Liberals is an example of what they try to do to him. They try to tee a counterintelligence investigation based upon a document that the opposing candidate, Hillary Clinton, paid for that they took to court to use to derail his campaign through, and create a Russia Collusion Investigation. This is not what happens in the United States of America. This is what happens in third world countries.

Gary: Exactly. And a special prosecutor that just doesn't want to hang it up either. I was reading some stuff this morning that my head was spinning, people that he's looking to indict right now or has indicted. It's absolutely crazy. Judge, how do people find your book or get ahold of you? I know Fox

News Justice with Judge Jeanine on Saturday nights, but how do they get your book?

Judge Jeanine: Well, they get my book at Amazon, Barnes and Noble, through my Facebook, there's a link on that, Judge Jeanine, and over jeaninepirrobook.com. You can get it anywhere. And it's amazing to me, but for anyone who wants to explain things, or is criticized, there's a tremendous number of footnotes, so you can support everything that you're saying. But in the meantime, I want to thank you so much for having me on this morning, and thank your listeners, and tonight on Justice with Judge Jeanine at 9:00 o'clock, Fox News, I'll be talking about the book again, and what happened at The View.

Gary: Judge, thank you for joining us. It's been a pleasure, and good luck with the book.

Judge Jeanine: Thank you. Thanks so much. Thank you.

4

COREY LEWANDOWSKI

Gary: On the line with me now is Corey Lewandowski. Corey and David Bossie, authors of Trump's Enemies: How the Deep State is Undermining the Presidency. They are also the authors of the blockbuster Let Trump Be Trump: The Inside Story of His Rise to the Presidency. Corey, welcome to the show.

Lewandowski: Well thank you Gary. Great to be on with you today.

Gary: So Corey, I've read your book. I bought the audio, and I've listened to that twice, and in some cases three or four times because when I read the book and listened the first time to the tape, it's hard to believe that we're not talking about a fictional story or a plot of a movie that's being made when you really understand what is going on in Washington today. And with that said, I've come to the conclusion that President Trump has to be made of some special DNA to be able to achieve the things he's achieved and put up with the crap that he's putting up with on a daily basis.

Lewandowski: Well I'll tell you what: it is remarkable. When Dave and I started digging into what took place during the Trump campaign and then continued while he was a president-elect and continues to this day by the people trying to undermine his presidency, if you told me this was taking place in the United States I'd said, "It cannot happen." If you told me this was taking place in a third-world dictatorship, I would've said, "I don't believe it." If you would've told me this was a spy movie, I would've said, "This is the worst plot ever" because it's unconscionable what has transpired.

Lewandowski: So let me just tell you in the quickest of terms what we know. We know that Barack Obama, when he was the president of the United States, expelled 35 Russians from the United States, and he sues for election interfering. Election meddling. Now when he did that, we were then the president-elect of the United States. And we asked for the briefing, the same briefing that Barack Obama had, so that we could see exactly what the material was that he used to expel these 35 Russians. For about three days they said, "We don't have the briefing, but what we're going to do is we're going to send you Jim Comey, Clapper, and Brennan, the three heads of the respective government agencies that oversaw this information. And we're going to do a debriefing, so you can all be briefed just once, one time in Trump Tower."

Lewandowski: So early January of 2017, the three of them come up, they give the president-elect a classified briefing, and then Brennan and Clapper leave the room, and Jim Comey, who's serving as the Director of the FBI stays behind, and he takes out a 30-page document, a 32-page document, which is now well-known as the fake Russian dossier. The one that the Clinton law firm Perkins Coie paid five million dollars to a British spy to go and get salacious material on Donald Trump from Russia. He didn't present in that information to the president-elect in the secured meeting with unverified information breaking every standard operating procedure of the FBI and of classified briefings.

Lewandowski: And the very minute he left, he then leaked that document as a document, which has now been presented to the president-elect in a secured meeting. And that's where this whole Russian investigation started and has continued to go forward since. And it is a total scam. There was no collusion. There was no cooperation. There's no coordination. I was there every single day. I didn't speak to any Russians. But this is the fake narrative that the media has perpetuated for the last two years now.

Gary: The media's perpetuated. And what? He has nobody by his side. Look, at least when Reagan was in office, Corey, he had some Republicans that were loyal to him. This guy, I don't know how he goes, quote unquote, to work every day knowing who you can trust and who you can't trust. And the Republicans are just as bad as anybody else.

Lewandowski: Well it's exactly right, and you've raised such a good point because I talk about this in our book. We say, "Donald Trump was a New Yorker, and he came to Washington, D.C., and he listened to the quote unquote establishment, and he started bringing guys into his administration who didn't support him when he was a candidate, didn't vote for him on election day, but weaseled their way into the administration to subvert the will of his agenda." And let me give you a couple examples: Gary Cohen, the former National Economic Chairman of the Economic Council. He was a Goldman Sachs president, didn't support Trump, openly supported Hillary Clinton, openly gave her money. He came to the administration, and he and Rob Porter, who is a staff secretary, were literally taking papers off of the Resolute desk where the president works, making sure he doesn't sign for better trade deals for our country. These aren't the Democrats we're fighting. These are our own people. And you look at the former Secretary of State, Rex Tillerson, he was a disaster.

Lewandowski: But the good news is we're finally getting rid of some of these guys, and we've brought in guys like John Bolton, who replaced H. R. McMaster, someone who hated the president more than he loved his country, but weaseled his way into the administration. We brought in Larry Kudlow to replace Gary Cohn. We brought in Bill Shine to oversee the communications department. These are professionals who understand what their role is, and while they disagree with the president on issues, which is healthy and important to do.

Gary: Good debate.

Lewandowski: When the final decision is made of what the path forward is, they implement it. And that's contrary to what the people who were working there were doing.

Gary: No, I agree with you. And I think he is bringing, finally bringing in, some great people. There was one part of the book though that I giggled, one I laughed to, the gentleman that was supposed to be in charge of putting together the cabinet that was on vacation when he was called. When the president wanted to start putting this together, he was not ready that created some problems for the administration right off the start because they were assuming they had people in place to take some of these roles.

Lewandowski: Well that's right. So his name is Bill Haggerty.

Gary: That's it, yeah.

Lewandowski: He actually held the same position during the Romney transition except on election night, he was actually at the Romney election night headquarters. For us on election night, he was like down in the Bahamas sipping Mai Tais and tequilas on the beach I guess. And we called him, "Hey Bill! We're ready to go now." It's the next day, he's one of literally a dozen people in the country who's going to staff the 4,152 presidential appointments that we have to staff immediately. He said, "I'll be back in about a week." Back in a week? "Oh where are you?" "On vacation." That was the mindset. These guys never believed in Trump, didn't think he was going to win.

Lewandowski: And so we were behind from day one, so you take the outsider in Donald Trump who had no friends in Washington, no huge political operation, when we won on election night, we had 200 full-time employees. 200. That's about the size of a big governor's campaign. That's about the size of a big Senate race. That's what we had on the campaign for a presidential race on election night when we won. Very small team, not everybody wanted to go into the government, and so we were behind from day one. And we're still catching up to this day. We've got 340 presidential appointments waiting for Senate confirmation right now because they haven't moved on it yet. And it is really stymied this president's agenda.

Gary: Yeah. And it's absolutely absurd. And I know we have limited time. I just wanted to ask you a couple questions. What do you think of Cohen's guilty pleading of the day?

Lewandowski: I have zero surprise about Michael Cohen's guilty plea. I've known Michael for what is four years now. He was a serial liar and a rat the first time I ever saw him. Nothing has changed with Michael except he's finally gotten caught. And whatever Michael has plead guilty to had nothing to do with the outcome of the election. Him not paying his taxes, him defrauding banks, him lying to Congress, all of those things are things that Michael Cohen did on his own, and I'm not surprised. And I think he and Paul Manafort, who's a very bad guy, who's been convicted and is sitting in a prison cell, are gonna be in jail for a long, long time and rightfully so.

Gary: Yeah. And you know what the shameful part of this is, and you know this, the mainstream media makes it sound like his conviction was based on something still to do with this Russian collusion. And there's nothing there.

Lewandowski: It has nothing to do with it. Here's the thing, Michael had nothing to do with the campaign. He wasn't a consultant to the campaign. He worked for the Trump organization. So whatever Michael did, he did it outside the boundaries of the campaign. He had nothing to do with it, and any lie that he told, which he's now plead guilty to on his own, no one told him to go to lie to Congress. That's never happened. No one said, "Hey Michael, go lie to Congress." He did that all on his own, and now he will pay the price because the only downside on this is Jim Comey's lied to Congress, no accountability. Andy McCabe, the Deputy Director of the FBI, lied under oath three times. We call that perjury. While the criminal referral has been there, he hasn't been charged yet. Hillary Clinton, Huma Abedin, Cheryl Mills all got immunity from Peter Strzok who him and his girlfriend Lisa Page were overseeing the Clinton investigation. This is the same guy, Peter Strzok, who interviewed Mike Flynn, who then turned around and said, "Mike Flynn didn't actually lie to the FBI." It's amazing that there are two separate sets of rules. One for the Clinton cabal and one for everybody else.

Gary: Yeah. And it's totally absurd. And quickly, did you happen to read I think Ann Coulter's column the other day?

Lewandowski: I did read Ann's column, yes. Yes I did.

Gary: Ann's a greater writer, but this one I found as a Trump supporter, I found it very offensive to tell you the truth.

Lewandowski: I know Ann. I know Ann very well. She has one issue that she cares about. It's the issue of immigration. And to Ann's credit, she has said that if the president doesn't build a wall, he is not going to get reelected. So I understand it. It is a pledge the president made, and it's a pledge he has to follow through on. But he needs help from Congress to do that. And it would've in my book, Trump's Enemies; we actually interview the president with the only book in two years.

Gary: I know. That was incredible.

Lewandowski: And we ask him about the Republicans in Washington, D.C. And this was right before the midterms, and he says, "They didn't fight hard enough." That's what he says in the book. He says they didn't fight hard enough for the immigration issue. And he's absolutely right. He can't do it alone. And if we had a few more people down there who were fighting for what they believed in and what was good for the American people, we'd be much better off.

Gary: And lastly, and then I know you have to go, the Mueller investigation. When is this going to end? This is absurd. It's frustrating on so many different levels. People are sick of talking about it. And when people read your book and understand what's really going on, they're really going to be aggravated, Corey.

Lewandowski: Well the Mueller investigation needs to come to a dramatic close. We asked the president about that in the book. I think it's in the fourth quarter. I think it's almost over. And we have now seen two years of an investigation that's cost the taxpayers somewhere north of $40 million. And the only crimes that Bob Mueller has found, none of them are related to what he was supposed to be initially investigating. So I hope when this is done, and I hope it's very soon, they make that report public at the same time that they have the rebuttal report which is being written right now because just because you're the prosecutor, doesn't mean everything you write is accurate. So we have to see both sides to this story, and if Bob Mueller has integrity, I hope he is following the leads which will lead him to the Clinton cabal and the Clinton team that actually tried to impact this election by using foreign sources and go after the people with badges at the FBI: Jim Comey, Andy McCabe, Peter Strzok, Lisa Page, Bruce Ohr who used their positions in the government to spy on American citizens on domestic soil simply because they didn't like their political beliefs. And if that would've happened to Barack Obama's team under George W. Bush, if he would've done that to Barack Obama, or somebody else, it would be called treason, and those people would be in jail for 100 years. But because it happened to Donald Trump, the mainstream media ignores it. And it's shameful.

Gary: Right. We're speaking with Corey Lewandowski. Corey, how can people get ahold of you or find your book?

Lewandowski: Best thing to do is go to barnesandnoble.com. Go to Amazon. Order the book today. It's been a great success, but I think it would be a fantastic Christmas gift. We can say Merry Christmas again. So you can go buy it, you can give it to people, and if there's something I can do to sign it, you can just get in touch with my office in Washington. I'll be happy to do it. But you know me, I'm a Massachusetts guy born and bred in Lowell, Massachusetts, as so many other people have been. And I am so grateful to live in the greatest country in the world, and I want to make sure from my children and God-willing my grandchildren we leave this country better than they left it to us because that's our responsibility, and that's why I fight every day to make sure Donald Trump is successful.

Gary: Corey, thank you. My producer does want to speak with you for a second, but I appreciate you taking the time joining us this morning. And it was a great book. Great job.

Lewandowski: Thank you very much!

5

DIAMOND AND SILK

Gary: On the line with us now is Lynnette Hardaway and Rochelle Richardson, popularly known and Diamond and Silk. They are American live stream video bloggers, social media personalities, and political activists, which we totally appreciate. They are known for their commentary and support of the United States and President Donald Trump, and they're here joining us today on the air to talk about Dummycrats.

Good morning and welcome to the show!

Speaker 2: Good morning, thank you for having us!

Gary: It's a pleasure having you. So Dummycrats looks like it's going to be incredible. Why don't you, first of all, tell the listeners a little bit about the whole movie and the process?

Speaker 2: You know, we know that the president is draining the swamp, so what we're doing is exposing the swamp and exposing the hypocrisy.

Speaker 3: Yeah. So in this movie, you will see Diamond and Silk going to these districts, especially the ones where these congresswomen are running around talking about, "We have to impeach 45." We go into their districts, we see how people are living in tents, people are homeless, yet they don't even live in that district. And they still are in a $4.3 million mansion on a $174,000 salary. So what we're doing is exposing their hypocrisy. We're giving you the truth with proof; we're not holding anything back. We're giving you the facts, and we're giving it all to you straight from the gate.

Speaker 2:   That's right.

Speaker 3:   But you can get your tickets at dummycratsthemovie.com. It opens nationwide in theaters on October the 15th. It's a one-night premier.

Gary: You know, what you guys are doing on a daily basis is what I feel most Americans think and feel, and people like myself appreciate it. The hypocrisy that we hear nowadays and the discontent and the constant fighting, and one of the things I did want to talk to you about, because one of our callers called in knowing you were coming on today, is Kanye West. What's going on with him right now, and how horrific CNN has treated him and the comments that are coming out about him just because he's expressing his opinion. It's shameful!

Speaker 3:   It's very shameful. You know, when you look at what's happening to Kanye West, we call what the left is doing to him, they're using what we call the Willie Lynch tactics to demean him, disparage him, to actually destroy him, assassinate him. Why? Because he's very influential, he can pull people off of what we call that Democrat plantation. He can wake tons of black people up and have them paying attention, and of course the left don't like that because see, the left feels like they own the black vote. Which they don't. And so once they destroy him in the eyes of all of his fans and followers, he will look weak. Those fans and followers, they won't be afraid to speak out or even they'll walk off that Democrat plantation. Those are tactics coming from what I call the gatekeepers. Because they don't want you to speak out, they don't want you to tell the truth. They don't want nobody to know they're actually in the black community, and in most of these homes, they are fatherless. There's no father in the home. People do need jobs.

Speaker 2:   They don't want you thinking outside of your box, of the box, the black box.

Speaker 3:   Absolutely.

Speaker 2:   They don't want you thinking for yourself and speaking for yourself they don't even want you knowing this for yourself.

Speaker 3:   Right! Right.   I don't mean to make anybody feel uncomfortable, but it's a slave mentality. Remember now, the Democrat party is the party of slavery, the party of Jim Crowe, the party of KKK. So look at how the party of KKK, they won't wear white hoods but today, the party with black hoods, trying to push socialism to oppress and suppress people. The more they oppress and suppress, what they do, they give you a few food stamps, give you an Obama phone, because they keep you quiet.

They do enough to keep you quiet but not enough to make a difference. It's time to start making a difference in these communities and it's time for the black race of people to propel forward instead of staying stuck in all of this foolishness.

Gary: Right. And that's what Donald Trump is doing. I believe he's trying to do, he's making things better for people, and look at its intimidation at that point on the part of the Democrats. They know they're losing the black vote, losing the Hispanic vote, and they're very concerned about it. I know we only have you for a little bit of time, but I want to throw out a couple of names and just get your reaction when I throw them out. Nancy Pelosi. What's the first thing that comes to your mind?

Speaker 2:   Nancy Pelosi needs to step down. First of all, we went in her district. Anytime you want to hand out plastic syringes and get rid of plastic straws, people on the street defecating in the streets, terrible! What are these people up here for? What are they doing? I'm tired of people working for their won greed and not the need of people. She's one of them, and she needs to be voted out.

Gary: I agree. Diane Feinstein.

Speaker 2:   Diane Feinstein, the Chinese spy. You know, first of all I think she need to be voted out. It's time for her to retire.

Speaker 3:   It's time for her to retire, that's right. To have Chinese spy for 20 years and you not know it makes me think something about you Feinstein. Who are you, and are you a spy? It makes you ask some serious questions, how you not know who's working among you for 20 years?

Speaker 2:   And not only that, how she took and exploited her with the rest of those Democrats, exploited Dr. Ford, and exploited her story. And now look once they done used her, you don't hear nothing about Dr. Ford.

Gary: How shameful is that, ladies? Think about that. I mean, never mind to the Cavanaugh family, to that woman, and to the country in general. Maxine Waters.

Speaker 2:   Maxine Waters she needs to go. She's been in office all of these years and hasn't pushed not one piece of legislation to help the American people, yet she's the main one running around talking about, "We have to impeach 45." It's time to impeach her, and maybe have her going somewhere eating on a peach.

Speaker 3:   That's right, and she living in a $4.3 million home outside of her district while people in her district live in tents.

Gary: And you can't get the mainstream media to discuss that topic, can you?

Speaker 2:   Oh no, they not going to sell that. They want to cover that up.

Gary: How about Robert Mueller? What do you think about him? What do we do with him at this point?

Speaker 2:   You know what? First of all, if the FBI took one week to investigate Cavanaugh, then this Russian investigation should be shut down. Because give us one more week! Just shut it down. Because there was no collusion. We don't speak Russian. If somebody came up to us talking about, "Hey, vote for this here person in Russia," we wouldn't have known it because we speak English.

Speaker 3:   We speak English.

Speaker 2:   I think Robert Mueller should step down. I think that this is a circus. I think that the American people are appalled by it. You keep an investigation going on for almost two years, and haven't found not one piece of evidence, but you dig so far. Any other thing that they find in somebody's past, "Oh, we'll use that." Especially the ones that dislike President Trump.

Gary: Right, it's a circus. How about Colin Kaepernick? Where do you think he lies in some of the things that are going on today?

Speaker 2:   You know, for him to think that it's okay to disrespect the flag, whatever you disrespect, your country, your flag, you're showing people it's okay for them to come over here and disrespect America. If he wants to kneel, how about kneeling down there in Chicago, where those people are at, where our black brothers are killing up our other black brothers? How about you do that? But here's the deal. If he wants to continue to kneel, you go right ahead. You going to kneel right on in the unemployment line.

Speaker 3:   And kneeling is not going to stop the crime, baby. Kneeling on the flag and disrespecting America, the anthem, is not going to stop the crime. You got to go where the crime is at. Go directly into the location. And that's what we saw Kanye West trying to do. Trying to go, have a seat at the table, let's talk about and discuss how we can help these different inner and urban cities. Whereas these other individuals like Colin haven't did anything. Kneeling on the flag is not going to do absolutely nothing because your message gets lost from kneeling on the flag!

Gary: And you know, Kanye made some great points when I stopped and listened to that session. When he talks about bringing jobs back into this country and helping the inner city, and looking at the ratio of violence and crime as these industries left the country. You know, when you look at that correlation, it is there and he's right. What's there not to like about that? Why are people dishing this poor guy when he says he wants to bring jobs back to America? Bring industry back to America? Get them in our inner cities? Get them working?

Speaker 3:   Because the left make their money off of poor black people. By you being poor, uneducated, and not knowing anything. See, remember, let's go back to when Obama was in the office. He gave you food stamps and an Obama phone. But look at all of the foolishness that he pushed. "Well see, I done gave you this so you can't run and fetch your mom. You can't say nothing." When people give you stuff, they

can control you. That's why it's best that you go and get it for
yourself.

Gary: Yeah, no I agree. What do you women feel about the Blue
Wave this fall?

Speaker 3: Oh, the only Blue Wave I see is Democrats waving goodbye
to the Democrat party, that they are tired of these left-
leaning liberals. When we saw what happened to Cavanaugh,
people were disturbed on both sides of the aisle. On both
sides of the aisle. How they took and tried to make a man
guilty, and he had to figure out how to prove himself
innocent, how they took the Me Too movement, politicized
that, and used that as a weapon to weaponize that against
somebody's impeccable record just to cater to assassinate
them? People was appalled by that. So you have some
people walking away from what we call the Democratic
party, the Democrat plantation, and switching to Republican
to vote Republican in these elections.

Gary: Yeah, and the story that's not being told is what you ladies
just said about many Democrats that were upset in the house
about how this was handled. Of course the media won't give
them any attention. I know we're getting right up against the
clock, so Donald Trump. When I say Donald Trump, what
first comes to your mind?

Speaker 3: I love him. He is one of the greatest presidents we've seen in
our country.

Speaker 2: Ever.

Speaker 3: I call him the new Civil Rights president, because he is sitting
down at the table, and inviting you to the table. What I love
is that he's not going through the Al Sharptons, the Jesse
Jacksons, the NAACP and the congressional black coffers.

He's going directly to the people, "What do you need? What do we want? How do we fix it? How can we fix it?" He's working on the justice system, the justice department, prison reform, so that hey, when you get out you can have a second chance. I want you to have a second chance, so you won't end up where you came from! I mean, I love that kind of stuff. We never, ever seen that in our history from any president, and they want to say Bill Clinton, oh he was the first black president. No he was not. He had thousands upon thousands of men locked up with that crime bill that he signed into law. But you know he did that for a reason, because him and his wife, they were taking money from these private prisons so he had to figure out how he was going to fill them.

Speaker 2:   That's right.

Gary: We're speaking with Diamond and Silk. Once more, give a promotion for your movie that's coming out? Let's hear about it?

Speaker 3:   Dummycratsthemovie.com. It's premier in theaters across the country on October the 15th, a one-night show. So we want you to go get your tickets, we want to see your face in the place.

Speaker 2:   And that's dummycratsthemovie.com.

Gary: Diamond and Silk, thank you for joining me this morning, and I hope you bring one of your shows up here to the Boston area. I'd love to see it.

Speaker 2:   Oh gosh, we will. Thank you so much and thank you for having us.

Gary: You're welcome.

6

DAN PERKINS

Gary:	On the line with me now is Dan Perkins. Dan is an Islamic historian, a nationally recognized expert on radical Islam. Dan is a foreign policy contributed to dailycaller.com, clashdaily.com, lifezeet.com, newsmax.com, and thehill.com. Dan is a master writer and author of The Brotherhood of the Red Nile trilogy, which centers around Islamic nuclear terrorism against the United States, and he's also the author of children's books. Dan, good morning and welcome to the show.
Dan:	That's almost not enough time left to talk.
Gary:	No, that's all right. First of all, if anyone hasn't read the books yet, The Brotherhood of the Red Nile, they have to because there's so much there, Dan, that has mimicked the reality of what we're going through. When I talk about it, it sends chills up and down my spine. It's crazy.
Dan:	I tell you, that's true, and thank you for that. But the newest book, Terrorist Gold, which is a continuation, and it's like people said to me, you can't leave us here with a trilogy. I said, "Yeah, but trilogy means three books." They said, "We don't care. We want more of the story." So I wrote this sequel called the Terrorist Gold, and just to put it in perspective for you, I wrote that book, finished the manuscript in the summer of 2015. And the premise and the story is the Russian involvement in the Democratic presidential candidate.

Gary: It's scary.

Dan: I know.

Gary: Very, very, very scary. But there's a few things I want to talk to you about. Let's start with this individual down in Florida. They keep calling him a bomber, the individual that sent the alleged bombs to the different people throughout the country here. Obviously a disturbed individual. I mean there's something that just doesn't smell right with this to me, nor does any of this that's going on recently. But we've got, going to different democratic politicians or operatives across the country. I was listening to Governor Cuomo and the New York mayor, and right away, they had no problem defining this as terrorism. Though, not too, was it last fall when that individual jumped the sidewalks, ran over a bunch of people? They refused to use the word terrorism because they weren't sure of the facts and situations. Just the hypocrisy sometimes is amazing. What do you make of this whole thing that's going on right now?

Dan: Well, that is a great question. And as always, thank you for having me on. I did an interview earlier this week in Chicago and I did something that I rarely ever do. And I mean rarely, maybe once or twice before in four years of being on radio. I had to correct the host. And it's a man that I've been on his show every week for two years. And I said to him, "Look, I apologize, but you got the facts wrong." And I said, "I think you're just being duped by the mainstream media." He used the word bombings, and I said to him, "No, they're not bombings, because bombings indicate that something went off and destroyed something, either a person or property. These were "bombs" that were found." So the fact that we got the bombs, as they're being classified, that they were devices where the timing mechanism was not connected, and on top of that, the casing, which normally in a pipe bomb would be cast iron or steel, was PVC plastic.

We don't really know. And apparently the timing mechanism was, in none of the 13 cases, was connected to the device. I don't want to call it a bomb because I don't think it was a bomb. So I think whoever did this, this is the guy who did it, and he did it on his own. It was clear that he wanted to send a message to these specific people who have been attacking not only the president but what the president stands for and what the president is trying to do for the country. And that's the commonality of all the people that were in this particular situation.

But the reality is, and, I've done a lot of interviews, Gary, since this thing started to happen, and I'm not asking you this question because I don't want to embarrass anybody, but I say to, rhetorically, how close for the bombs to Bill and Hillary Clinton's house in Chappaqua?

Gary: They weren't even near it.

Dan: Nobody knows. Miles and miles and miles away. Same thing with Barack Obama. They're intercepted at the post office. And so, were any of these people ever in danger? No. Were other people on the Republican side in danger? Yes. All those representatives and staff people who were physically confronted in restaurants with people yelling and screaming. We have no idea of how close some of those people were to physically harming senator Cruz or Gillibrand or whoever. And so there is not, as Hugh Hewitt tried to tell us yesterday in one of his tweets, that their equivalent, that these bombs are equivalent to the confrontation with Mitch McConnell or Ted Cruz or whoever. No, they're not. Because the person who did this never came in contact with any of the people that he was sending this message to, and the bombs never made it to those people. So I disagree with the left that's trying to say that they're equivalent. They're not.

Gary: They're having a field day by just using certain terms. That's why I refuse to say bombing, and you know a word, the misinformation of that word, they can use it, it allows them to use the number of different ways. Never mind, Dan, the shooting at the baseball practice a year or so ago. You want to define a terrorist attack; we can say that's real one-on-one confrontation right there.

Dan: Yeah, no, I've written not about this particular bomb threat, but I've written about the midterm, and I put out a warning in that, I think that was done on a News Max. What I basically said, Gary, and I think it's important, we saw what happened in 2016 when Donald Trump won the election and beat Hillary. We had riots in the street. I believe that the democratic leadership has hyped the Democrats for the last year or so about this big blue wave coming that's going to lead them to take over the house and possibly the Senate. I said, and I cautioned the American people, "If, in fact, there is no blue wave and the Democrats do not get control of the House, I fully expect after the midterm elections, people to die." Absolutely believe that.

Gary: I am with you 100% it's similar to a message that I've said a number of weeks in a row on this show. I don't think we've seen anything until after the election and the outcome of the election. And that's when you know what will hit the fan.

Dan: Yeah, and you and I must be the only people talking about it, because I can't find anybody else raising that question. And my publisher said was it was a great message, a message of warning, but I really believe, and if it turns out to be a red wave, where not only they don't win the House, but they lose, physically lose seats in the House. I had a gentleman, two people that I heard on the radio earlier this week who are projecting more aggressively than I am, one was projecting 58 Senate seats, another was projecting 62 Senate seats, and one was predicting a pickup of four seats in the House and another one was projecting a pickup of 12 seats in the house for the Republican Party.

I think that there are things out there that are already happening with the Republican turnout swamping the Democratic turnout in early voting. That's going to be problematic for the Democrats. And I think that that the Democrats have nothing offer. And I think when the people walk in the voting booth on, that's a week from Tuesday, I've got an ad that's running in about 280 markets across the United States on Monday and Tuesday, and it's basically a 30 second ad that I paid for that basically says, before you walk into the voting booth or your check a box on your voter ballot, ask yourself this one question, "Are you better off today than you were two years ago?" If you are, vote Republican. If you're not vote, for somebody else. We're the Republican Party. We stand for you."

And that's going to run in 280 markets across the country Monday and Tuesday, I think 12 times during the morning drive. Because I want to remind the American people, hey, there's a reason why you're voting. And what is it? Is it because you want to impeach Trump? Or is it because you want to continue what Donald Trump has started and makes sure that he has a House and a Senate that can work with him.

Gary: Dan, we're going to take a quick break, but when I return, I want to pick up the conversation a bit about the possibility to violence, because there are a lot of articles being written by Democratic operatives now that lead me to believe that that plan is already in motion. You're listening to Business, Politics, and Lifestyles. My name is Gary. We'll be right back.

We have Dan Perkins on the line. Dan is an Islamic historian and nationally recognized expert on radical Islam, as well as an author.

Dan, I've been reading a lot of articles from Democratic operatives that are sort of warning, putting the warning out that if we lose in the midterms, then we know that the system has been fixed against us. Which is misinformation and dangerous rhetoric. But I think that that thought process already in process, because they know what's ahead for them.

Well, that's a great point. I heard something last night. Fortunately I was lucky enough to have recorded it, and I heard it in my car, and then I went back to the house and was able to pick up part of it. It was a reporter writing the story about the midterms. And it was an interesting perspective because he was doing an oral commentary, and he said, "Well, you know, we on the left believe that the outcome of the November, 2016 election was interfered with with the Russians and it wasn't a legitimate election. In fact, Mr. Trump doesn't really represent the American people."

But he went on to say, "If, in fact we do not gain the House, we have to rethink the outcome of the 2016 election and the 2018 election. Because maybe what Mr. Trump is saying is what the American people believe." And so that was the first time I'd ever seen a person on the left question that if the outcome isn't what they expect in the midterms, that they may have to change their thought.

Now, I also heard yesterday something similar to what you're talking about where the Democrats have already set up the excuse for not winning was because of the caravan coming north and the Kavanaugh hearing and now the bombs. It basically skewed the results because it provided a false narrative for people to make a vote against the Democratic Party. So there are, you're right, they're already trying to build up. I mean, isn't it amazing? They went from a landslide massive blue wave to take control of the House to now backing off, that that the election is going to be suspect, not true representation of what the American people think. I mean they're unwilling to admit that they've got the wrong message.

Gary: Right. And I think the gentleman that you're referring to, with what he said, that's the tone they have to take in order to correct themselves and move forward with a story that the American people are going to believe in and ideas that the American people will want to buy into. But when you get, I'm sorry, but the Pelosi's, the Schumer's, it's just never going to happen with that group of individuals. They're hatred toward Donald Trump, that's where they're coming from on every angle. They think they're going to get in. Going to get in there and remove him from office instead of dealing with like the ad that you're placing. Are you better off now than you were two years ago? And I think that is the question to be asked, once again.

Dan: Right. I've recently reminded a host on a talk show that I broke a story almost nine months ago when I predicted that, and I wrote an article about it on News Max, that the Democratic Party is the party of victims. And I said that the person who's going to be the nominee for the Democratic Party will be the ultimate victim. The ultimate victim in the Democratic Party is Hillary Clinton. And they laughed at me when I said that nine months ago. They're not laughing at me today because they're talking about her as being a legitimate candidate in 2020.

Now I said in the article when I wrote the prediction, there are two exceptions. One, she has a health crisis and she can't physically handle the run, or two, this is where midterms become very important, if the Democrats do not get control of the House in 2018, after the election, look for the Justice Department to wind up with a new leader. Sessions will retire or leave or resign. And we will then have a new Attorney General who will open a legitimate investigation into the Clinton Foundation, the transaction on Uranium One, and he's got to look at the Clinton emails. So she could be winding up in an orange jumpsuit. That's why she couldn't run. But short of those two things, she's going to be that the candidate.

Gary: It's funny you say that, because I read that, when you had written that, I read that to a friend of mine and I'm like, "You know, there's some truth to this." He said, "No, no, you're absolutely crazy." And matter of fact, I'm going to pull that out again and run it by him, because when I looked at it, I said, "Bingo," because that's the way that the foundation was being built here. She's the perfect victim, let's run her again. She'll go in there. But I agree with you. If we take them both and we don't get rid of Sessions, I think we have a bigger, another problem in this country, because we have to clean up some of the mess. That's the other thing; a lot of these operatives think they could. They just think they could do whatever they want and there's no accountability for it, Dan. How do we, as a country, allow that to go on? It's so wrong in so many different levels.

Dan: It's because, and it's interesting to see what's happening in the body politics in the United States, how the traditions are beginning to unwind. I've written and talked about many, many times about the Democratic playbook, which was given to every Republican senator or congressman or president in the last 40 years, that this is how they're supposed to act.

When we attack you, you're supposed to agree, you're supposed to go hide in a corner, resign or whatever, but we're in control. And they've run that playbook for 40 years. And the Republicans have not had the spine to stand up. All you have to do is look at John McCain and look at Mitt Romney, how they ran against Barack Obama. They refuse to get in his face. They've refused to go after him, so the playbooks that you can't do that. We can do it, but you can't do it. That all changed when Donald Trump became president because he took the playbook and threw it out.

Gary: Rightfully so. Rightfully so.

Dan: What we're dealing with is the fact that we're now seeing more and more Republicans in the House and the Senate. I mean, here's the perfect example, Gary, of the Democratic playbook. All 11 Republicans on the Senate Judiciary Committee decided they were not going to question Dr. Ford. They brought in an outside person to represent that. Can you imagine 11 US senators sat there and watched that woman interview Dr. Ford and they never asked a question. That is the example of the Democratic playbook.

Gary: Right. Yeah, it's totally outrageous. And we're getting to the top of the hour. I do want to just get your position on this. They call it caravan, we call it invasion, invading force. Well, how do you think this is going to turn out and is it helping or hurting the president, what's going on there?

Dan: I've written a piece on that and I basically said, "Look, here's what I think the president needs to do. He needs to create a 10-mile zone away from the border. After that 10 miles zone, anybody that comes across that border in that neutral zone, when that happens, we shut down all 48 legal crossings for anybody or anything coming into the United States, which means those 48 official crossings produce about a billion dollars in revenue to the country of Mexico every day. So we're going to shut down the border. We're going to deploy the troops, which the president now is going to do, and we're going to bring in the aircraft from the air force and we're going to bomb that 10 miles zone and we're going to fill up with a massive craters. We're going to make it even more difficult. And when people come into that zone, the official borders close, we concentrate all our efforts on looking around at what people are, because we'll use spy satellites and drones, and we'll deploy our soldiers and border patrol and buses and trucks and take those people back. And if they come back, we'll put them on an airplane and send them back to their country."

Gary: Dan, we're at the top of the hour. How can people find you?

Dan: Danperkins.guru, G-U-R-U, is all you need to know.

Gary: Dan, as usual, thank you and I look forward to speaking with you again soon.

Thank you. It's always a pleasure to be with, Gary.

Dan: You're welcome.

7

DR. CORSI

Gary: Our next guest on the line with us is Dr. Jerome, excuse me, Corsi. Dr. Corsi is the author of the best-selling book Killing the Deep State: The Fight to Save President Trump.

Dr. Corsi received a Ph.D. from Harvard University in political science in 1972. He's an investigative journalist and senior staff writer for several conservative websites, and he's the author of six New York Times best-selling, including the number one best sellers Unfit for Command, great book, and The Obama Nation, another great book.

Dr. Corsi, welcome to the show.

Dr. Corsi: Great to be with you. Thank you very much.

Gary: Yeah, it's great to have you here this morning.

So you reveal the secret plan to destroy Trump and as you say the deep state will not care if Trump is removed from office by impeaching him, declaring him mentally incompetent, or in the final resort by assassinating him, as long as he's removed from office before the completion of his term.

There are some that may have read that at one point and said, "Dr. Corsi is just great. Great writing for his book. Great information." But as we see what's really unveiling and falling apart over there in Washington, your statements look truer and truer on a daily basis, Doctor.

Dr. Corsi: Well, thank you. I wrote Killing the Deep State to show you the compelling evidence that within the FBI there was really this coup d'état plan. It's very shocking that the goal was to deny Donald Trump the ability to be president. And if he did happen to win, which we now have evidence some of the top members of the FBI consider to be a tragedy, they were going to do everything they could to find an insurance policy to remove him from office by impeachment. And it's pretty shocking, but the evidence is compelling.

Gary: You know when you hear that, the first thing when I read through your book I'm saying to myself what other times has this happened in American history, Doctor? Or has it happened?

Dr. Corsi: I don't think it's ever happened. The point of making Killing the Deep State is that this is unique in American history, that there's actually a legitimate and documentable coup d'état plan that someone not serve as president.

And the FBI, the Justice Department, the CIA all seem to be working together to try to develop this Russian collusion theme as the basis on which Trump was going to be denied to run for president. It didn't matter there was really no evidence for it, or that Russian collusion is not a crime. There's no crime against Russian collusion.

The thing is so preposterous. What is shocking about my book, I think the average person reading it is going to be really floored is the extent to which this hatred of Donald Trump has created I think a treasonous situation within what I call the deep state, these entrenched elements within the bureaucracy.

Gary: And the hatred, I mean we've hated other presidents or president-elects, whatever the case, and the hatred towards Trump from my point of view is like I have never seen before.

And a lot of times when you ask people, never mind in the government level of it, but what they hate about him, they're not really even sure which is even scarier to me.

Dr. Corsi: Well what I point out in Killing Deep State is we've gotten to a point now where the left has so gone to the far side. I mean it's now almost a socialist-style European party. The hatred of Donald Trump is intolerant. In other words, the hard left, what I'm beginning to call the hate left, does not want any opposition to its ideas. It doesn't want a First Amendment, certainly does not want a Second Amendment, and even the Fourth Amendment, searches and seizures, the hard left is seemingly comfortable with a social media that is intrusive, knowing everything about us and just as long as it can censor conservatives and silence the speech of Libertarians the hard left is okay with that.

Gary: Yeah, they're fine with it.

Dr. Corsi: I was saying, that to me has never happened before in my lifetime. I never thought it would happen in the United States. This is not the Democratic Party of John Kennedy or Hubert Humphrey. This is an extremist party that is happy with Antifa as its enforcement arm.

Gary: Exactly, exactly. So Dr. Corsi did this come to fruition during the Obama administration? I mean, this just doesn't happen over night. Maybe it did happen overnight but, or is this something that's been brewing in these agencies for some time and Donald Trump was just the guy that they were going to enforce in their mind not to allow him to be elected?

Dr. Corsi: Well the argument they make is that they increasingly, and probably going back to George H. W. Bush, the bureaucracy has been globalist. I mean these are people who are largely leftists in the bureaucracy hired and living in Washington D.C.

Their view is we should have no borders, that we should have this international globalist free trade, that we should be party to these international organizations like the United Nations. The United Nations wants to take the guns away from everyone. You walk into the United Nations compound and there's a picture of a revolver with the barrel of the revolver twisted into a knot.

These are the kinds of, that the hard, hard left. You see it I guess in California. You see it in different parts of the country that are really just so different from the mainstream of American politics. That they're intolerant. I'm not going to get interviewed by the mainstream media, by ABC, NBC, CBS.

Gary: Right.

Dr. Corsi: They don't want people to read Killing the Deep State.

Gary: No.

Dr. Corsi: It has too much truth in it that the hard left does not want the average American to know.

Gary: And most of us or a lot of people believe that when you talk about who controls this country, a lot of people's first reaction would be, well of course, the president. The

President of the United States, he's the guy in control. But that's far from the truth isn't it?

Dr. Corsi:
It is because one of the shocking things for a president when you come into office is that the bureaucracy, these hard entrenched, and we now have these what we call the SCF. These are the special executives since Jimmy Carter. There's like ten thousand of them, top managers in these various departments that can't be fired at all unless you really eliminate the department. They're grandfathered even above secret service.

You've got a situation there where the president realizes he gives an order and the bureaucracy comes back and says, "We're not going to do that. We have other laws in place and we're going to basically subvert your policy. We'll take you to the court."

Gary:
We've seen it.

Dr. Corsi:
Look at what's happened when Donald Trump has tried to enforce immigration laws. He's up against California saying, "We're a sanctuary state and we'll take you to the Supreme Court to argue our right to be one."

Gary:
Yeah, and the Attorney Generals throughout this country know this and they're using it in their favor to subvert things like immigration law that the president's trying to get through. So it's frustrating I'm sure for this administration.

But the other thing you say is this is the deep state, but the deep state is still getting stronger and stronger. So even with a guy like Trump in there, there's no way for him to slow this down or eliminate this deep state?

Dr. Corsi: Well I've said that Donald Trump is probably the one who has the best chance to do it. He's going to need the support of a large section of the American people. But what I think is coming, and when I talk about it and explain to people which is very important to understand in Killing the Deep State is that this is a propaganda attack against Donald Trump. In other words, you can't beat propaganda with the truth so you say well there's no evidence of Russian collusion. You only indicted, Robert Mueller, 13 Russians who won't come back and face trial, can't be extradited. The Justice Department says they did not influence the election. Trump did not coordinate with them.

Well this hard core says well you just haven't looked hard enough. We keep looking we'll find or make up the evidence of Russian collusion. And now they're into making it up. They're trying to blame Roger Stone who has repeatedly shown that he had nothing to do with the leaking or the breaking into the Democratic computers to get these emails that WikiLeaks produced. This is the big rub that the Democrats are basing their Russian collusion argument on.

So it looks like that was done by Seth Rich, an internal job. Analysis even published in The Nation, which is a left leaning journal by NSA experts say that this breach of the Democratic National Party computers was done inside job and it was quickly done, and it had to be somebody like Seth Rich. But that doesn't convince anyone.

So Donald Trump's going to have to counter attack to save his presidency, and he's beginning to do it. I think my book predicts in the next period of weeks and months you're going to see the tables start to shift and it's going to be the Democrats who are going to come under investigation for the real Russian collusion.

I write two chapters in Killing the Deep State to show you that it was Hillary and John Podesta who were being paid by Russia.

Gary: Right.

Dr. Corsi: And that they were lying. I even give you the Russian oligarch names who were paying Hillary through the Clinton Foundation and Podesta through some shell corporations the Russian oligarch organized criminals figures close to Putin set up to pay him and offshore entities you can document through The Panama Papers. All of this was hidden and secretive. If Hillary had won none of it would have come out. We find the evidence of it in the WikiLeaks, which is all these emails that were so damaging.

But as I point out in Killing the Deep State, the American public is going to have a hard time hearing this. The deep state has gotten worse. Okay so now James Comey's book is going to come out on top of mine, and he's going to present himself as the victim. In other words, he was in a higher honor. Well, James Comey three times did this FISA court application to get electronic surveillance on Donald Trump's campaign. And he used this Fusion GPS dossier, which he knew that the FBI could not validate or authenticate as true. And when Comey testified to congress, and he's asked about it, he said, "Oh that document was scurrilous. We couldn't prove it."

Well then why did he take it? He's either lying, committing some kind of what looked to me like a crime taking it to the FISA court.

Gary: FISA court, yup.

Dr. Corsi: Or he was lying to congress. This is a guy who the mainstream media's going to try to make out to be a hero.

Gary: So Donald Trump, if he starts to unmask this deep state, once you start this process if the president starts it, there's no return. I mean the people that you're going up against and I think Trump's probably the only guy that could do this, but there's some very powerful people and organizations you're going to have to go after and that's an undertaking in and of itself. But from my perspective, Doctor, there's not return once you start.

Dr. Corsi: Well this is the point. I think Donald Trump is the only person I know of that could do this. But Donald Trump just this past week fired some of his legal counsel and brought in Joe diGenova.

Gary: Right.

Dr. Corsi: Now I've known Joe diGenova since 2004 in Washington, and he is a former US attorney. He's a very tough, professional and honest law enforcement officer, now attorney.

His wife Virginia Toensing, also a very, very top Washington D.C. attorney. Her client, William Campbell is the lobbyist who turned state's evidence in this proving that there was Russian bribery in the uranium industry that was before this Committee on Foreign Investment in the United States voted to give the rights to Russia to buy this Uranium One company that Hillary and Bill Clinton had arranged to sell to them while Hillary was Secretary of State.

And Mueller, Robert Mueller, and Rod Rosenstein, number two today in the Department of Justice, covered up this Russian bribery evidence because they didn't want the

Committee of Foreign Investment of the United States to know about this. If that committee had known about it they might have not allowed Russia to buy Uranium One, which got 20 percent of the US uranium, some of which was shipped to North Korea by the way.

And in all of this Hillary Clinton made the Clinton Foundation 175 million dollars. Now I think President Trump is going to say it's time to get a grand jury called and investigate this bribery screen that was suppressed. That could put under subpoena for criminal investigation Robert Mueller and Rod Rosenstein, both of whom I think would have to resign.

This is the beginning I think of what Trump is organizing counterattack and the evidence we have from the inspector general-

Gary: Right.

Dr. Corsi: Is only a little piece of what this inspector general has found. I think it's going to show the deepest, most shocking corruption, just like I document chapter and verse in Killing the Deep State.

Gary: Right.

Dr. Corsi: This corruption is going to become known to the American people in the Trump counterattack, which is coming.

Gary: Yeah. It can't come soon enough. And even some of the cabinet positions that he switched around this week I think personally were good choices and I think he's going to do what he has to do to protect himself because there's no one else out there protecting him but himself.

Dr. Corsi: Well and when Trump first came in he had not any experience at the top level of Washington and he trusted, for instance, Reince Priebus and the GOP establishment to help him get Obamacare repealed and replaced. When they failed he fired Reince Priebus, which he should have done. And then he adds this Goldman Sachs group in with Rex Tillerson-

Gary: Right

Dr. Corsi: And Secretary of State Gary Cohn as economic advisor. Well they did not approve of Donald Trump pulling out of the Trans-Pacific Partnership or imposing these new tariffs on steel, which will bring back the steel industry to cities like Cleveland and Pittsburgh.

Gary: Amen we all need it, yup.

Dr. Corsi: More like a revival, right. So Donald Trump got rid of the Goldman Sachs group that he doesn't need. I've known him for decades in New York, and I've known him quite well, and he has always run his companies with a small number of people who are loyal. He's appropriately asking, "Why do I need these people. I don't need this many people. They're just going to be a nuisance. They leak. They are not loyal to me." It's very tough in Washington with this deep state entrenched as I point out in Killing the Deep State. I know it's going to shock people but there's very few that Donald Trump can call on in Washington who don't want to destroy him.

Gary: It's absolutely amazing and from your perspective where is ex-president Barack Obama in this chain of command.

Dr. Corsi: I present compelling evidence in the book that Obama is really still active.

Gary: He pulls the strings.

Dr. Corsi: Wizard behind the screen.

Gary: Yup.

Dr. Corsi: And he and Valeria Jarrett, who has moved into this mansion that Obama bought in Washington, are really daily doing everything they can to undermine Trump's presidency behind the scene.

Gary: Amazing. Dr. Corsi, where can people get a hold of you and where can they get this great book?

Dr. Corsi: Well thank you. Killing the Deep State has now become number one on Amazon. It's about to be I think one of the best-selling books of the Trump presidency every written, is Killing the Deep State: The Fight to Save Donald Trump, and it's in bookstores everywhere now. It's all across the country in bookstores. Any bookstore you go into you'll be able to find Killing the Deep State. Just look for my name, Corsi, C-O-R-S-I, and it's on amazon.com, barnesandnoble.com, and booksamillion.com.

Killing the State is now readily available across the country. Jerome Corsi, C-O-R-S-I, is my name.

Gary: Well Dr. Corsi, as usual it's a pleasure speaking with you, and as this thing unravels I look forward to speaking with you again.

Dr. Corsi: Thank you. It'd be a great pleasure. Thank you Gary.

8

ROBERT SPENCER

Gary: We are now joined by Robert Spencer. Robert is the director of Jihad Watch and the author of the new book, The History of Jihad: From Mohammed to ISIS. Good Morning, Robert. Welcome to the show.

Robert: Great to be here. Thank you very much.

Gary: First of all, very good book that you have written there, and I want to get into it, but sorry about the little delay. We've had a little hot conversation on a horrific incident that occurred here in Massachusetts this week. Unfortunately, it's occurring all over the country with what's amounted to the execution of a police officer. A very sad, sad situation.

Robert: Yeah, it's terrible.

Gary: Terrible. So I have people asking me all the time, Robert, what is going on with ISIS? Why don't we hear anything about ISIS or hear more about ISIS? And I don't have the answer. I do make the assumption that this administration is giving ISIS what they truly deserve.

Robert: Yeah, absolutely, Gary, ISIS controlled a territory larger than Great Britain when Donald Trump became president. Now, it essentially controls tiny enclave here and there and it's on its way out. The problem is that doesn't mean that it is dead yet. The ISIS Group had attracted 30,000 foreign jihads from a hundred different countries. A lot of those people are dead now, but a lot of them have been dispersed. A lot of them have returned to their home countries, including the United States, Great Britain and several countries in western Europe. There are several hundreds of them walking around free in Great Britain because the British authorities have decided, I think, in a disastrous error, that they don't pose a threat. These guys have not changed their minds. They've not changed their worldview, they've not changed their outlook, and they are free, and they're in our countries. We have not heard the last from them.

Gary: No, I don't think we have. How many would you guesstimate are in the United States of America and where are they?

Robert: Many fewer.

Gary: Much fewer.

Robert: So 20 or 30 and I can only hope that they're being kept close watch on. But nowadays you never know. It may be that the FBI is too concerned with trying to find evidence of Russian collusion to keep track of them. I don't know.

Gary: Yeah. Because we always hear there are only so many agents, so many people they can put on things. So if they're putting their resources into the wrong pot, we're all in trouble in regard to that. So your assessment of the way that President Trump is handling the war on ISIS?

Robert: Well, I'm all for what he's done, he's decimated their holdings in the Middle East. It looked as if at the end of the Obama Administration, as I show in the book, that this group was going to be around for generations to come and was even starting to become legitimized. It's recently been confirmed, what has long been suspected, that the Turkish government, which is supposed to be our ally and Syria, also bought oil at bargain prices from ISIS, which controlled at its height, 60 oil wells in Iraq. And so it could have been because it was useful to the neighboring state around for decades or more, but Trump has made it so that it's pretty much a thing of the past except for the unfortunate likelihood that they're going to be lone-wolf jihad attacks in the United States and in the UK and in western Europe.

Gary: When you alluded to the fact that they sort of disappear and reappear, that is always my concern. And what about, Robert, some of these concerns you hear about? The newest thing I've been reading about, it's not new, but it's more and more I read about is the use of drones. That their use of drones to attack us, whether it's with a chemical weapon of whatever the case may be. How real is that?

Robert: Oh, it's very real. These people, it's kind of a funny thing because a lot of people in the West often thinks that these Islamic Jihad movements are throwbacks, that they're rejecting all of the modern age, and they want to run around and kill people with scimitars and so on. And we certainly, actually, there are a lot of stabbing attacks, machete attacks, that kind of thing. But ISIS, in particular, and Al-Qaeda to a lesser degree, have always been very, very eager to use absolute cutting-edge technology and to exploit, particularly in terms of communicating on the Internet, extraordinarily sophisticated techniques to do so. And so they're certainly worth looking into the use of drones. As a matter of fact, the jihadis, the Palestinian jihadis in Gaza have already started to do that in setting fire to thousands of acres of Israeli farmland by sending drones over with Molotov cocktails attached and so on.

Gary: Yeah, I have been following that, and I don't think people in this country and maybe around the world realize what is going on over there and what they're doing and how they're inflicting these drones or whatever they're using to get over there to start these fires. But it has to open your eyes and make you aware that this could happen anywhere in this country or anywhere around the world and we have to be ready for it. But we talk about ISIS and neutralizing them from a military point of view, but doesn't it go beyond that? How do we get to the mindset? How do we get to those? I'm amazed at how many individuals sign up by reading their propaganda online.

Robert: Oh, yeah, Gary, this is the biggest omission, the biggest failure of the entire defense against the global jihad since 9/11 and this is one of the main reasons actually why I wrote this book because people don't realize that there is a unifying ideology that the Palestinians and ISIS and the people who took down the World Trade Center on 9/11 and to the Fort Hood shooter and the Boston Marathon Bombers and so many others, they have the same worldview, they have the same belief. They are working on the basis of a violent expansionist ideology that is the premises in nature and is going to keep coming. There are many people who still believe it among Muslims, and they are going to continue to be attacking us. It's a much larger problem than just ISIS or any other particular group. It is an ideology that is rooted in Islamic texts and teachings that has to be addressed by all people of goodwill, Muslim and non-Muslim. And there has been really no effort to do that in the time left.

Gary: When the president and people talk about whether it's illegals coming into your country and sort of diluting the fabric of whether it's this country, the UK, I think there's something to be said about that. And from the perspective of, I've talked to individuals that are in this country, probably not legally, that have very nasty things to say about this country, and you'll ask them why they are here, but they'll immediately start talking very positive about groups like ISIS, which blows my mind and one point and is very concerning to me, Robert, on the other part on the half.

Robert: Well, it ought to be, it's extraordinary. But it's true that when the immigrants are vetted, in general, they are not, of course, Trump has called for extreme vetting, but these things have not generally been implemented so far and he has so much resistance within the government. When immigrants are vetted, there is generally no serious attempts made to determine whether they have jihadist sentiment. And a lot of people are coming in who are actively hostile to the United States and they're not here to become Americans and they're not here to get a good job and take care of their families. They are here because they want to ultimately bring down the American system by means of terror attacks so that it can be replaced by a system based on Islamic law.

Gary: And in the book, in your book, The History of Jihad: From Mohammad to ISIS, I mean there are a number of takeaways that I want to get into it with you, but we're led to believe that this violent segment of Islam is something that's new, which is so far from the truth. And I just wonder, those that spew that information, and they're not necessarily Muslims concerns me, Robert, because they should know if you read it. First of all, if you make a statement at least look into the history of it before you make the statement. But they're hell bent on saying, "No, this is just a fragment that's new and it will pass. It's not going to pass." It's part of their fabric.

Robert: Yes, and this is what I show in the book. This is actually one of the main reasons why I thought it necessary to write because people don't know this history, and they do think that this is just some reaction to the state of Israel or to the foreign policy of the United States and that it's not something that is common throughout or constant throughout Islamic history, which they think is characterized by peace and tolerance and magnanimity and multiculturalism. As a matter of fact, on the other hand, in reality, the history of Islam, from the beginning, is characterized by jihad, by conflict with non-Muslims all the way through Islamic history. Obviously, not every Muslim ever pursued this but because it has justification within Islamic texts, there has always been jihad conflict between Muslims and non-Muslims for 14th century's and I detail it all in the book from Spain to Africa to the Middle East to Iran, to India. It's always been there.

Gary: Right. And to the present day situation where the same thought process is taking place that did hundreds of years ago.

Robert: Yes, exactly. The same ideology as I was saying before that ISIS and the Palestinians and all these others, that's the same ideology so also people who believe those same things that they must wage war against non-Muslims and subjugate them under the rule of Islamic law have always existed since the beginning of Islam and have always started conflict against non-Muslim.

Gary: Yeah. And it's rampant around the world and the fact that, as a society, we don't want to believe the history of the truth I think says a lot about what is going on in society today. Maybe we don't teach enough in our schools and maybe those teaching don't know enough or don't want to bring the facts across. But when you become a society that does not want to deal with facts and your book clearly states, is factual. It states it out over a period of time. But if you want to ignore those, you doomed, Robert, sooner or later you're going to be doomed.

Robert: Yes, absolutely. As the old saying is those who do not remember history are condemned to repeat it and that's exactly what we're looking at now. We think that it's going to be different somehow in our contacts with the Islamic world, even though there's been conflict between the Islamic world and non-Muslim entities ever since Islam began and somehow and most Americans don't think that this is going to happen again and yet there's never been a reformation or a rejection or reconsideration of any of the Islamic doctrines that have given rise to the conflict. Why should we think we're going to be immune?

Gary: Yeah. And your book gives us a great understanding of the geopolitical situation occurring here in the 21st century and, hopefully, I think, ultimately formulating strategies to defeat this radical Islam and I think-

Robert: Well, the first thing we have to do is understand what it is and acknowledge that it is something that's deeply rooted in Islamic texts and Muslims who are genuinely against this kind of violence and conflict need to address this and work for genuine reform.

Gary: Callers on this show or people that you speak with, that's one of their biggest frustrations is they don't feel that enough Muslims speak out about the radical Islamic terrorists.

Robert: Actually, Gary, they do speak out. There're always condemnations of terror attack from Muslim organizations whenever they occur. That's actually the only thing that they do. What's the big omission is that there is, believe it or not, there is no program in any mosque in the United States right now to teach young Muslims why they should reject the understanding of Islam that is taught by al Qaeda and ISIS and other groups like them. And so that's the problem is that they, condemnations, are easy. But what is difficult is the actually trying to do something against these groups. And that's what we're not seeing.

Gary: Yeah. And if we don't come up with a solution to this, I mean, look it's not, it's been going on for hundreds of years. It's not going to stop. They want to challenge our way of life. But from your perspective, can Islam be reformed?

Robert: Well, I think it's actually going to be very difficult because you have the Koran teaching warfare against unbelievers. You have the Koran. The Koran says a law in the Koran, "To this day, I have perfected your religion for you." Well, it's perfect. You can't fix it. It ain't broken to start with. And so I think that also the history of reform in Islam is a sign that it's going to be very difficult. For example, in 1985 there was a Muslim reformer in Sudan named Mahmoud Mohammed Taha. And he taught that the peaceful passages of the Koran should supersede the violent ones. Usually in mainstream Islamic theology is that the violent passages should supersede the peaceful one and he was hanged as a heretic by the Sudanese government. So this does create some impediments to reform. If you're going to get killed for calling for reform, it's going to be pretty hard to affect reform.

Gary: No, I agree. And, Robert, how can people find you or get your book?

Robert: I have a website jihadwatch.org, which is updated many times daily with news and commentary about jihad activity and all its forums all around the world. And the book is available now for pre-order at amazon.com and barnesandnoble.com and on August 7th, just a couple of weeks now, it will be available at any self-respecting bookstore.

Gary: Very good. And the emails that you send out on a regular basis, and when I open those up, and I look at different situations across the world that are involved in, whether it's terror attacks or Islamic groups, one has to read that to keep abreast what's going on in the world. Because every time I read something somewhere else in the country, my fear is, "God forbid, when is this going to happen in this country here?" And it's amazing how much the mainstream media just doesn't tell us about how many of these attacks and things that go on.

Robert: Yeah, absolutely. And there's a deliberate policy of omission of the motivating ideology because of the idea that somehow if we speak about these things as having roots in Islam, it will make people be angry with innocent Muslims. And there's no reason why that needs to be true. Obviously, no attacks against any innocent people are ever justifiable. At the same time, if we're not informed about what we're dealing with, we're never going to be able to deal with it properly.

Gary: No, I agree. Well, Robert, it was a pleasure having you on the show this morning, and I look forward to your book. I've read some excerpts of it online and have you back on as time progresses here.

Robert: Hey, thanks. Call me anytime.

Gary: Thank you, Robert. The fact of the matter is we're led to believe that Islam it's a peaceful religion and this is just something that's just occurring. It's a new wave within the religion, and it's so far from the truth. That's why when you read his book, read some of the excerpts until the book comes out that you'll see that it's far from the case. And no, I'm not going to sit here and condemn a group of people or anybody, but radical Islam is a problem. It's still a problem across this country. It's a problem across the world. And it's again, a situation that you have to come up with solutions. We can keep pointing the finger and making comments about it. But I am very pleased that this administration is doing what they have to do to defeat it as he said at the beginning of the conversation.

I just think it's so important what the president is doing, and the less we hear the mainstream media talk about it, I think the better off we are because that leads me to believe that they do not have any clue or idea of what the president is doing that is purely top secret. Whereas the Obama administration would tell groups of people the date, the time that they're going to inflict harm on them to make it look like they were doing something. And we know how that turned out.

So, Robert Spencer, the name of the book, again, The History of Jihad: From Mohammed to ISIS and once it is available, I think you should read it because as he said, it's not going away. That ideology is out there. It's a mindset that has to be changed, so we can be defeating them on the battlefield. It doesn't necessarily, we're defeating the mindset and with some of the propaganda that is online right now and individuals that sign up and leave this country to go fight on a battlefield somewhere else. It's just you and I would never think of that shame like, "what are you talking about?" But there are people that are doing it. I would hope when they come back to this country, at least under this administration, that they're either being watched or detained or whatever the case is to make sure that we're safe.

But in countries like Great Britain, they allowed to roam the street and when you're allowed to run the street, and you have not, to me, it's no different than an alcoholic, or a drug addict until you change their way of life and their mindset, they're a potential danger. And I think in Great Britain with that many people roaming the streets with that mindset, there is quite a bit of danger out there. So, I mean, we just got to keep our eyes open and keep aware of your surroundings and make sure that we know what's going on. But to Robert Spencer, an expert at a minimum, get onto his website and sign up for his weekly newsletter. I mean you read articles, it's happening in Germany or even in Australia, things that this group is still carrying out that our own media is not telling us, which is just another issue. But you'd need to be aware that it's still going on.

But we are fighting the fight, and we are knocking them back, which is what we want to do. Unfortunately, there must've been a mix up with the senator this morning, because was supposed to join us. Because I did want to talk to him about a number of things on the state-level including the rainy day fund, the Red Flag Bill and other things that we talk about, and we never find the real answer to our school system and school security and things that are going on in that regard. But I do have some other members of the state Senate that will be joining us in the next few weeks to talk about those issues. Geoff Diehl will be joining us to talk about his race against Elizabeth Warren, which is turning out to be it's going to be an interesting fall here in New England. We have been trying to get the Senator Warren on the show. I've talked to her staff. I'm not making much headway there, and I think that's apropos of the way the senator decides who she will speak to and who she will won't to speak to. I know anyone who listens to this show, I do have my own political beliefs, but I try to be fair. I want anybody of any political belief to come on and state what they feel and no one will ever be hostile to them because that's not what we want. I think, again, we'd be hypocrites if we did not allow those with opposite beliefs to get on here and tell us what they think. And maybe we all could learn something by that, by them, but we're going to keep working on it. I'm not going to let go until I physically could get the word, "I'm not coming on to your show."

9

ELENA MARIA LOPEZ

Gary:	On the line with us now is Elena Maria Lopez. Elena is an immigration fraud victim, current whistleblower, and citizen advocate. In June of 2018, Miss Lopez identified and presented a series of national security immigration fraud cases to the White House.
	Elena, good morning and welcome to the show.
Elena:	Good morning. Thanks for having me on, and I actually went to the staff of the White House last week.
Gary:	Did you really? So I want to talk in this couple segments we have, I want to first give you the opportunity to tell our listeners. I've listened to your video, read a number of things. If you could give them an idea of what you're talking about. In your experience, what brought you to this position?
Elena:	It happened to me personally that somebody used me for a green card. I thought I was happily married, and then two years of marriage to the day, he admitted he had only used me for a green card. He told me this straight to my face. Just quickly signed the divorce papers. I think I have my green card. I'm going to be a US citizen, and was boasting. And when I filed for a divorce and refused to sign any further immigration documents, because I was his sponsor into the country, that's when he became violent. And he tried to kill me, repeatedly threatened me, and his behavior was so shockingly different than the previous time I had known him, I said, "Huh, what's going on here?"

And then I started noticing financial irregularities. He had filled out credit in my name. The lease on my car had changed. There were a lot of shady things all converging at one time, and that's what got me into investigating, hmm, who did I really marry? Despite me thinking that I properly vetted him, I obviously hadn't, and then as I started digging deeper because he was still threatening me, by the way, and trying to kill me. He came at me with a firearm.

I had to hire a retired FBI agent for help during my divorce, and we found out the government didn't properly vet him either. He should've never been allowed into the country because he was involved in large scale criminal activities, drug running, drug production, money laundering, car theft, a lot of really shady things in Holland, and he bypassed background checks. Why? Because he was marrying a US citizen. And despite me documenting things with this retired FBI agent, and basically handing them everything on a silver platter, saying, look, we also found out he lied on his visa to enter the country. He lied on his green card application. Easily, they could've cherry picked any of it and said he's clearly deportable, and a violent criminal, and of safety to this US citizen and possibly the country, they have done nothing.

Gary: Wow. And how did you meet this individual?

Elena: I met him through a friend while I was finishing up college. If you meet somebody through a friend, you feel like that's at least one stage of vetting, that it must be a nice guy.

Gary: And eventually you brought this to the authorities, or was it that the FBI come and talked to you? What help was the government in all of this at this point?

Elena: Oh, no help. The FBI never got in touch with me about my own case, only about the national security cases I discovered down the road. But the FBI just says, "We're going to wait for him to do something really criminal in this country." Department of Homeland Security says "We see cases like this all the time." The immigration investigator actually said, "I'd be a rich man if I had a dime for every time I heard this type of story." And when I went to my US senator, he called it a marriage dispute. My US representative said he didn't get involved in whistle blowing, but in the same breath volunteered to help me sponsor someone else into the country.

So I was appalled because, meanwhile, I'm doing the research, and I found out that fraud was rampant for legal green cards, and the government was doing nothing. It was an open secret amongst themselves. They knew it was rampant. They never warned US citizens, and when the US citizens do find out, were given no level of protection.

Gary: Yeah. Having listened to your story and read your story, I talked to someone yesterday about exactly what you're talking about. What fraud is going on in regard to this behavior and in regard to getting into the country and get married? And he said the fraud aspect is one thing. The violence that we don't hear about against the people that sponsor is totally out of control, and at crisis level, and nobody wants to deal with that right now. Nobody wants to deal with that. I think this administration's dealing with it, but none of the politicians want that on their plate right now.

Elena: Oh, definitely not, because the security loophole I discovered was actually through domestic violence legislation, that if you claim to be a crime victim or a domestic violence victim, with no evidence, no interviews, and no investigations, you can get fast-tracked green cards and citizenship, no questions asked. And your immigration paperwork is taken from a regular path and diverted to this special social work path, where people don't have the proper training to do investigations, and vet cases, and deal with fraud. And those are the national security cases I discovered. I literally tripped over them because I started seeing so many cases that looked exactly the same, and people were using this green card method and citizenship method to bypass background checks, hide criminal activities, all of that kind of stuff.

And then they quickly remarried, active military, with high level security clearances, usually living on US bases. And one of the first case, I was like, whoa! By the second and third case that I saw and each case involved two US citizens at least being defrauded, so you see one foreign national using this method, and then a second, and then a third, and then a fourth, and you're like this is a pattern. Somebody's writing a guidebook on how to pull this off.

Gary: Yeah, and you brought up a great point. It's amazing if you look into this how many men file complaints against someone like yourself, that they abused them, and it changes the whole tone of them coming into the country. The whole procedure changes.

Elena: Yeah. Actually, I found out based on government regulations, I'm the abusive spouse.

Gary: Right, right.

Elena: Do you like that one? He tried to strangle me, has repeatedly threatened me, and came at me with a firearm, and I'm the abusive spouse. You want to guess why? I'm emotionally abusive because I refuse to sign off on his immigration papers. He was eligible for a fast-tracked green card, and once that happens, they're not even allowed to interview me. They're not even allowed to accept my evidence, and we think that's what happened.

Gary: Before I want to talk about your testimony, how did you get away from this individual? He was out to kill you, and you hired an ex-FBI agent to help you, but how did you get away from him?

Elena: I had to flee the state of Pennsylvania, and I had to go back to New Jersey. Part of my family is in Massachusetts. Hi, Massachusetts. Hi, Dad. I had to flee back to my mom's home state of New Jersey, and the state of New Jersey put me in hiding because they figured my safety was so compromised based on the evidence I submitted.

Gary: And, not that you may know, where is he now?

Elena: He's living in my old house outside Westchester, Pennsylvania, right outside Philadelphia.

Gary: Yeah, I know the area very well.

Elena: He's living openly and freely. He might even be a US citizen by now, and I'm still in hiding with help from the state of New Jersey. In 2016, Department of Homeland Security investigators called me into their office in Philadelphia, warned me that he was dangerous, that I needed to protect myself, but they still would not open an investigation or deport him. So they had me in tears, but then they're like, "Yeah, we're not going to help you. We're just going to warn you that he's dangerous, but we're not going to help you, the US citizen, in harm's way."

Gary: So any of you listening out there that think, well, this is just Elena's story, and it's a one-shot type of deal, you really need to go online and look into this. Because I've done this, knowing that you were coming on the air, Elena, and it is, like I said I'd consider it almost epidemic proportions, Elena, throughout this country.

Elena: It is, but, by the way, I'm a Democrat. I can't get anybody from my own party to even return my calls, let alone sponsor legislation to protect US citizens in the immigration process. And so, yes, I agree that this administration is the first administration to actually step up to the plate on this issue.

Gary: Rightfully so. The administration's obligation is to protect its citizens, protect American citizens, and, look, we all know that the whole immigration process is a scam and a fraud, and it needs to be overhauled. And the fact that your elected representatives are concerned more about their next vote than they are of your safety should be alarming. It doesn't matter, Democrat or Republican, why people should be voting the right people into office, that they're going to protect them, because you never know what's going to happen to you, a family member, or a friend.

Elena: Right. And the media wants to make this such a contentious issue, that if you speak out on this, you're obviously racist. Or you're xenophobic. And that's not the case because I'm a biracial Puerto Rican. My dad's a black Puerto Rican. I'm from New Jersey. We have a very diverse state. We have people that are first generation Indians. We have biracial people. We have people that are defrauded by people from their home country. So we have such a diverse pool of victims, race isn't even issue. It has to do with criminal activity.

Gary: So when you hear them constantly talk about you're a racist if you question something like this, your blood has to boil because you're the person they do not want to see out promoting the cause, because they can't throw that race card at you, Elena. They may try, but they really can't.

Elena: Yeah, and that's why I also openly said, look, I'm a Democrat, and by the way, I could show you Russian nationals defrauded from Russian nationals. I can show you African-Americans defrauded by other Africans. So I have the evidence. I'm never going to expect anybody to take my word for it, and it's the same thing on my case. I never asked anybody to just say, "Look, take her word for it. She said she was abused by her Dutch husband. Just take her word for it." I meticulously gathered evidence, and I think that's where the whole false allegations for a green card is really dangerous is that we're not given due process or investigations, and that's dangerous.

Gary: Now, clarify, was this during the Obama administration, most of this took place?

Elena: No, actually, it was during George W. Bush administration, and his administration was no help at all.

Gary: No, look, George W. Bush, I think a lot of his true colors, when you hear stories like this, are coming out. You know, Elena, we're going to take a break. When we come back, I want to hear a little bit about your testimony. You talk about false allegations, because you have some great stories of some cases you talk about, and I want our listeners to hear it. You're listening to Business, Politics and Lifestyles, and my name is Gary.

We're speaking Elena Maria Lopez. Elena is an immigration fraud victim turned whistleblower and citizen advocate.

So, Elena, thank you for being here. I listened to your testimony, or at least part of your testimony, and I want to know reaction. What came about from that testimony?

Elena: Nothing.

Gary: Yeah, I mean, that was the impression that I got. "Thank you for coming and telling us this horrific story, and see you later," basically.

Elena: Yeah. And try and do it without totally breaking down and crying, and having a mental breakdown.

Gary: Right, right. Exactly, because it's an emotional topic for you.

Elena: Right. Right. So, sadly, nothing. The only thing that could remotely come out is I've now documented the case, because to even get to that level, I had to go through six weeks of vetting and evidence collection, and the Senate Judiciary Committee can directly pull immigration files as an oversight committee. So they could show that I'm not lying, and that my evidence is credible, and that everything I said on the record was accurate. That's pretty much the only plus.

Gary: So they did nothing. What was your feeling going into this? Did you anticipate maybe they're going to do something? Or this was the end result that you thought would happen?

Elena: For me, it was about speaking out, and challenging legislators about how the laws really work. So I don't have any regrets, but that said, I still was taking a risk. I had to check in with my police department and let them know there was a heightened risk to my safety, and all of these other types of things. I had to let my neighbors know who I really was, and if they saw somebody like my ex-husband or anybody coming after me, they needed to call 9-1-1. So I had to do all of those personal things, but I think it was so important to speak out because politicians aren't willing to listen to US citizens that are defrauded.

Gary: Right. Yeah. When I listened to you speak, hearing you live on the air and having listened to some things on file on the internet, you're to some degree in a witness protection program as a victim of a crime, which is absolutely absurd.

Elena: Right.

Gary: Absolutely absurd.

Elena: Right. And rather than protect me, the feds have actually put me in greater danger because when I reached out after the testimony for President Trump's new crime victim office for immigrant crimes, rather than helping me, they refused to help me because they had to protect my ex-husband's privacy rights. They then released all of my personal information over the internet into the media.

Gary: Yeah, that's just absolutely insane.

Elena: So my information is now out there, so once again, for the third time, I had to update my emergency safety plan. So that kind of stuff is really scary.

Gary: Have you reached out to the president, the administration directly?

Elena: Yes, I have, and that's where I went in with the false allegation cases. I brought a series of false allegation cases that I vetted with a team of other whistle blowers and a retired Department of Homeland Security investigator, and that's when we showed that, look, this looks like simple domestic violence legislation, but there's major national security loopholes within it. They're not taking any action now, but I'm still hoping to basically light a fire under their butts.

Gary: Yeah, and as much as you can, I think you have to keep it going because the way the news cycles work today, if it's not in front of them on a regular basis, something else will take precedent.

Elena: Right.

Gary: Let's talk about September is False Allegation Awareness Month. How important is that?

Elena: That is very important because organizations like SAVE, where you can find out about this on saveservices.org. They did a survey to show that one in 10 abuse allegations are false. Where would we put up with that kind of track record, where one in 10 surgeons kill their patients or something like that? That's a pretty bad track record. And we know all the traditional reasons for filing false allegations of either abuse, sexual violence. I'm not saying they're all false. We need to take real victims seriously, but we know the ones like if somebody wants an upper hand in child custody or in their divorce, they will claim false allegations. That's been well documented in the press. Some investigative reporters have poked around on that.

And then we have the Nikki Yovino case. She was just sent to a year in prison for making false allegations against two college students, and it was because she was trying to get in good with her new boyfriend, and not look like she was promiscuous. We all know the Brian Spanks case. You know that one?

Gary: Yeah.

Elena: His accuser came out and admitted that it was false, but she really wanted the $1.5 million settlement that she was suing the school for where it allegedly happened. So people know of all of those types of incentives, but nobody knows about the immigration incentive for claiming false abuse status.

And I think that's really important during this month because it is False Allegation Awareness Month.

Gary:	Right. Yeah, and these particular cases, when you look at how these students, their lives are ruined, and the fact that the colleges immediately jump. The victim is, okay, we believe everything you say without really getting into the investigation, and those being accused pack up and leave. The fight is on to clear their names. Especially, some of these young athletes that did nothing wrong, who potentially looking at college as maybe a stepping stone into better things. Not just their education. Some of them are looking at professional sports, and once this hurdle is thrown in front of them, it's all over. It's just incredible. You're right. We have to get out there and let people understand that this False Allegation Awareness Month is very important.

And from the side that you're talking about, you know what, Elena? A lot of our listeners probably didn't even realize until they heard you today that aspect of it from the immigration point of view and getting your green card.

Elena:	Yeah. Very few people know about it, and people usually, their first contact with me is when they're facing some kind of allegation in local court, and they're saying, "Wait a minute, this doesn't make sense. What's going on?" And then they do the research in terms of trying to prepare their own defense, and they find out about this immigration loophole.

Gary:	Right.

Elena:	And we're not talking about uneducated people. I've had attorneys contact me. I've had public defenders contact me. And the attorneys sometimes were contacting me about their own cases. So I've had some very well educated people all of a sudden in these horrible situations in an emergency, trying to scramble to defend themselves. And I think that's important, but there needs to be a fine line. This is not going to be easy because you should not assume the victim's wrong, as in my case, and you shouldn't just assume they're 100% right either. Like I said, investigations are key. Collecting evidence, figuring out was it really Nikki Yovino or Elena Lopez making up these stories, or are they really in harm's way?

Gary: Well, nowadays, the political correctness aspect takes the side of the victim, and we've had experts come on this show to talk about how that whole investigative process has ended. The investigator should listen to all sides, take the information, and then come up with a conclusion, not just come in there biased, taking the side of the alleged victim. The fairness doctrine is gone at that.

So if you could come up with one thing to start fixing this process, is there any one thing that you think needs to be done immediately?

Elena: Investigations.

Gary: Yeah, I'd agree.

Elena: But on equal footing. Equal investigations. I suppose in the immigration process, and for when you're accused of any kind of crime, it's the investigation and not automatically saying the victim, but saying the alleged victim.

Gary: Right, because terminology persuades the mindset of people. The more they hear a certain term. Instead of alleged victim, just victim, if they keep hearing victim, they're going to think right away there's no doubt. A lot of people are naïve to think that the investigation has been done, never mind the fact that the investigation is not done.

Elena: Right, and I'm not discounting the Me Too movement at all because I'm the perfect candidate for Me Too because you have people for the last 20, 30 years who have been ignored, like my case, and they need to speak out because they're like, "Look, I couldn't even get my DA or my local police to even investigate," or maybe who they work for just kind of shut them up quickly and told them to shut up and put up.

So the pendulum is swinging both ways. We need to find that middle ground. That is so important.

Gary: So where should my listeners go to just read about this type of information or maybe read about your case? I don't want to put any of your pertinent information out there, so you tell me.

Elena: Oh, that's fine. I make sure that I'm just generally New Jersey. It's all good. In terms of False Allegations Awareness Month, go to saveservices.org. They have a lot in terms of the campus and all of the other types of false allegations and fixes and stuff like that. For my case, you can just laugh. This is New Jersey. I'm in New Jersey. You can go to Yo Lopez. That's the easy version of my site. Just think, "Yo, Lopez!" Go to yolopez.com, or immigrationfraud.com, and if people really want to do something about this, call your US Senator, call your US Representatives. Say, look, we demand that national security loopholes be taken out of domestic violence legislation. That is so important, and I have that information on immigrationfraud.com.

Gary: Elena, it was a pleasure speaking with you, and I'm going to follow this as time goes on. And, hopefully, at some point, we can have you back and we can have some good news for our listeners that things are going in the right direction because, as we both just talked about, this is an issue that has to be dealt with. Hopefully your ex-husband leaves. I still can't believe he's in your home, but that's a whole 'nother story. That's frustrating enough. He'll just go on his way, and let you live your life because it's insane. When I think of the fact that you're in hiding and he's openly living in your ex-home outside of Philadelphia, I think it's mind-boggling. I think a lot of people listening to this show are going to be outraged over what's going on here.

Elena: Yeah, I hope so, because I would really like to have my life back and not be in hiding. I really want to be able to use my name openly where I live.

Gary: All right. Thank you, Elena. It was a pleasure speaking with you, and I look forward to talking to you again.

Elena: Thank you.

10

DONALD STINSON

Gary: We have a guest on the line with us this morning, Donald Stinson. Donald is the author of "Downstairs at the White House" and I chuckle when I say that because I read his book this week and were gonna talk to Donald about this book. He's the former senior vice president of the newspaper division of Gnat company Inc., and Donald welcome to the show.

Donald: Well thank you Gary, good morning.

Gary: Good Morning and sorry about last Sunday, the flu had the better part of me last weekend.

Donald: I just hope you're feeling better, I went through it myself.

Gary: Yeah, I am feeling much better. I thought I was gonna skip through the winter, good portion of the winter without it but it found me and won for that weekend. It's all in the past, but I received a copy of your book the other day and was reading through it. A number of things came to mind, but I've got to ask you a couple questions right off the bat.

Donald: Sure. (laughing)

Gary: 17-year-old, how does a 17-year-old get a job-First of all I was thinking if I was to get a job in the White House under which administration would I like to be there and I think under yours under the Nixon administration I think you had it on all ends, an interesting time but how did you get this job in the White House and you claim, you state you were not an intern. You were working in the White House.

Donald: Right, well first of all, It was all by accident. Friends have told me from time to time that I have a little bit of Forrest Gump in me.

Gary: (Chuckles).

Donald: And I just kind of stumble into things. The short version of a long story is that I went to, I got into a program that allowed me to go from 11th grade into college and I got into American university in Washington.

Gary: Wow.

Donald: And so I started there right at what would have been my senior year of high school. Obviously I was very young at that time and I ended up meeting a, say meeting a guy who knew a guy, who had a job in the old executive office building as a clerk and didn't want to continue. Back in those days, you could kinda put yourself through college and I was doing most of it and so I needed a job. So I interviewed for it, I got the job but I was such a moron that I didn't realize that I actually worked in the White House complex for the first several days, a buddy had to point it out to me. I don't really know why I didn't put it together when I could actually look out the window and see the west wing of the White House but I didn't realize that I was in the complex that included the White House.

Gary: Yeah and this wasn't a summer job, this was a year round job while you were in school?

Donald: Yeah, I was an employee. I was not an intern.

Gary: Unbelievable.

Donald: And I had top-secret security clearance, matter of fact, I did important stuff like getting coffee.

Gary: (Chuckles)

Donald: And making copies and carrying and delivering mail and carrying things around, things like that for which actually you do need a security clearance. Because most of, a lot of the materials were classified.

Gary: We joke about it but what you are speaking of is the way that you really sometimes learn to work your way up the ladder as they say, and understand how business and in your case business and politics may have worked at the same time. So you took this job-first of all impressive that you jumped a year of high school right into college and you took the job at the White House if you don't mind me asking, what was the pay you were getting for this job?

Donald: I made right about I think it was 3, a little under 3 dollars an hour which actually was in 1973 when I started there that wasn't bad at all. Typically, not for a college kid and so I think that would probably equate to about maybe 10 or 11 dollars an hour now.

Gary: Right.

Donald: And you know it was a good job. I worked full time and I went to school full time and eventually I started working for an assistant to the president who actually was a descendant of the Busch family of Anheuser Busch. Fascinating guy who had been a WWII pilot, fighter pilot. Actually he, his name was Peter Flanagan, he was behind largely behind Americas use- development and use of the space shuttle.

| **Gary:** | Really? |

| Donald: | Yeah, and so I worked there for a while and then one day I literally, literally ran into a guy in the hallway who was filling up a percolator with water at at water fountain, and I knocked him and the water all over the place. He turned out to be one of Vice Presidents Agnew's speech writers and we got to be friends and eventually one day I asked if there was a chance I could work for the vice president, and he helped me do that. Now when they interviewed me for a job which ended up being in the correspondence section, there was thee answer I gave them in an interview, and there was the truth cause they asked me why I wanted to work for the vice president and my answer was because I think he might very well be the next president of the United States. He was at the top of the Republican Party at that time Spiro Agnew. |

| **Gary:** | Right. |

| Donald: | And this is had nothing to do with Watergate just the fact that 1976 was approaching and he was at the top of the pile. Then the truth of the matter was is that I had by that time turned 18 and what I thought it would be is just cool because- |

| **Gary:** | Right. |

| Donald: | His office was down the hall from the one I worked in. It had these really cool flags. The vice presidential seal over the door and two big guys with guns whenever he was in there. I just thought it would be cool and I ended up having a very fun and very interesting and unusual time there. |

| **Gary:** | Great. You know it, when reading through the book there's some very comical moments but when you think of the period that you were working with, working in this |

administration and as you say, eighteen months was it eighteen months into this after receiving your first paycheck, you know all hell basically breaks loose in the White House-

Donald: Right.

Gary: You're having this fun and you're not sure, if it sounds like you're enjoying it but all of a sudden reality hits you in the face. So when it did start, when hell did start breaking loose here what was some of your first thoughts as to what was happening? What was going down here, I mean, it's hard to even place yourself in that position.

Donald: Yeah(laughs) the first thing that happened of significant note, well, well first thing. The White House at least back in those days, was very similar to any other office that you worked in. I mean you run into people all the time, some of them in this case were known on a global basis, were certainty in the news media as it concerned Watergate As that was developing. I spent allot time in 1973, delivering very inconspicuous envelopes to thee, republican members of the senate. Back in starting in May 1973 the senate Watergate committee, Sam Mervin.

Gary: Right.

Donald: Of North Carolina hitting it, convened and there was some communication going back and forth. I had no idea what it was, I had no intention of opening anything up and looking at it. At that age my concern was What if my dad found out that I had looked at something like that?

Gary: Right.

Donald: It would have killed me. I was more concerned about that than anything else. But you know, so that started then when I moved to vice President Agnew staff course he ended up resigning.

Gary: Right.

Donald: And that was, it was really a horrible situation. You can say what you want about the things he was charged with and everything else and frankly all of those things are legitimate. However, I got to know him a little bit. I got to know one of his daughters and his wife much better. Utterly charming people. So very nice and you know it hurt. It hurt to see what they were going through. I talk in the book about what it was like going to their home with some things that we were given after he resigned. Taking some things to his home that were personal items and Mrs. Agnew just breaking into tears. I mean there is a real human element that ends up in these things. But anyways so I was in the room when it was announced that Vice President Agnew resigned. Which was a-if I may divert just a second-

Gary: Go ahead, yeah.

Donald: There's a strange story to this one. I would not ever claim to be physic but every once in a while, I think we've all had dreams that end up kind of coming true one-way shape or form. Agnew resigned on October the 10, 1973. The night before I had been asleep, I guess in the early hours of the morning I had a dream and the dream was is that a woman I knew who was a secretary, as they were called in those days. She was actually the secretary to the guy who was Bob Hopes nephew who worked on the staff. She and I were standing next to one another and all of a sudden her mouth just fell open.

Well the next day, actually I was supposed to have classes. I wasn't supposed to come into work for a while. Something was canceled and I ended up going down to the office and at around noon time, one o'clock something like that we were all asked to go to show up in the vice presidents conference room. While we were all cheering this on because we thought this is, he's going to be cleared of everything and everything's gonna be great. All of a sudden the door flies open and it is the vice president's military aide who comes to the top, the front of the table in the conference room, throws down some papers and says "Our leader has just resigned his high office" and did a bout face and walked out the door. My friend who I was standing, I was indeed standing next to her mouth dropped open.

Gary: Yeah. Right.

Donald: So did everybody else's. Those are weird circumstances because you didn't even know how to answer the phone after that.

Gary: Right. Right.

Donald: Those sort things happen. After I left Agnew's staff which I hope in read mail, which was one of the funniest things I've ever done in my life Gary because. We used to get mail from people who, there was a guy who sent in a five-page letter every week to the vice president.

Gary: (Laughing).

Donald: I've never understood it. Call entitled cranberries, Americas silent hero. You look this up and go "Gee-Wow, that's interesting". There was a woman who had a family somewhere in the Midwest who thought that she and her children were cranially   wired by the martians that was the term she used. They had, they wore literally little tin hats and she was nice enough to send one to vice president Agnew.

My book is made up of things that are poignant and funny and then just plain weird. One of the poignant moments actually had to do with something we received there and it was a garbage bag. Course I was a kid so anything anybody doesn't want they put on my desk. I opened this thing up and it was addressed to Spiro Agnew Washington. In it were these little tiny pornographic pictures that had been cut out with scissors that had been thrown in. Broken electric scissors and there was some claws that looked like they may have had blood on them, so I freaked out. I took them down, I took this thing down to the secret service. While I was down there there was an agent who I knew who said Don Let me introduce you to Mr. Hill. I said Okay, great. Shook hands with him, I wasn't really paying attention. I was mostly looking for food at that age.

Gary: Yeah, Exactly.

Donald: The agent says to me "Hey dummie- you don't know who that is?" That's Clint Hill. And Clint Hill for many of us who are history fans and old enough to remember the Kennedy assassination remember that Clint Hill threw himself on the back of JFKs limousine in Dallas on November 22, 1963.

Gary: Right. Yup.

Donald: For my money, no one ever out heroed Clint Hill. He's still alive, he writes some wonderful books and fascinating stuff. A great American hero. A week or so, ten day something like that later I happen to be in the west wing of the White House on the elevator and I got on an elevator all alone with John Connolly, who'd been the governor of Texas.

Gary: Wow. Yeah.

Donald: Who had been hit by the so-called magic bulled. There were lots of these odd things that turned into very interesting things typically for a kid who was a history nut. Anyway when we were done with, after Agnew they found us jobs. I got sent over to HEW, where I ended up having to, which is now HHS. I was sent to a job there believe it or not I had to resign in order to get

paid. It's in the book, its one of those weird kinds of things. My life's like that Gary.

Gary: Laughing. That's all right, I'm gonna hold you right there for a second were gonna take a quick break. You're listening to Business, Politics and Lifestyles were talking with Don Stinson author of "Downstairs at the White House"

On the line with us now is Donald Stinson. Donald is the author of, "Downstairs at the White House." You know, Donald, what interaction, if any, did you ever have with the president himself?

Donald: Well, I had interaction with both President Nixon and President Ford. I was there through part of the Ford administration. Just to put it into perspective, after I had to quit in order to get paid, I ended up back in the White House and I was a messenger and a clerk working out of the East Wing in the White House proper. I had a little cubbyhole down in the basement, where the title "Downstairs at the White House" and I was really downstairs at the White House. Although I was a goofy kid, I wasn't completely stupid, and what I used to do is I would come in in the morning through the West Wing, in order to have an opportunity to pass President Nixon as he went from the residence into the Oval Office through the rose garden, so I could get my big kick for the day by saying, "Good morning, Mr. President.

One day, as I came through, I had a book about Theodore Roosevelt, and there was something that he noticed. I guess he saw the cover, and he stopped me. To say that we had a conversation, Gary, would be kind of overstating it. I had a pulse and I think he wanted to talk to somebody. It wasn't really a conversation. I stood there and listened as my knees kind of shook.

But he stood there and talked for, I don't know, several minutes at least about Theodore Roosevelt, about Winston Churchill. It was one of the great moments of my life. And I have to say again, you know, you look at Watergate, and you look at the mistakes that were made and everything else, but Nixon was brilliant.

Gary: I was going to say, a very brilliant man.

Donald: Incredibly so. I have yet to ever find, including other presidents that I've had the pleasure of meeting over the years, I've never felt that kind of voltage from any other human being. I mean, that was something special, and it was a terrible shame how it ended. My interactions with members of the First Family, I mean, by accident one day I confused Mrs. Nixon with a maid in the president's residence.

Gary: Oh, my God.

Donald: She kind of set out from a darkened area, which is near the elevator, the family elevator. It goes up to the family floors. Something like, "Hi, kiddo." And I just went, "Hey, kiddo. How you doing?" To which I caught holy hell afterwards, because I should not have been calling the First Lady, Mrs. Nixon, she, on the other hand, was so incredibly gracious about it and she got me out of trouble.

Gary: I was going to ask you about the Nixon family and the kids themselves, how they were. You know, you read so much about him. It's hard, and you had a first-hand view.

Donald: Well, the only one I didn't know, and may never have met, was Trisha and her husband, Ed Cox. But, the Eisenhower's, David and Julie Eisenhower, I had spent some time with. In fact, a couple of times I had an opportunity to play a baseball game, it was a card game, both back in those days. A baseball with David and some other people that got pulled into the thing.

These were just incredibly nice people. I mean, they really were. You know, Mrs. Nixon was made out to be a certain way in Oliver Stone's movie about Nixon. She couldn't have been any nicer. She was a lovely, charming lady and I could have never had any complaints about the way that they conducted themselves in any way. They were a class act.

Gary: As we get to the bottom of the hour here, can you give us one or two quick funny moments in the White House?

Donald: Yeah.

Gary: I mean, you had a lot of them, but-

Donald: Yeah. Well, first of all, I just have to put in a plug. The book is available on Amazon. You can even buy it for as little as $4.99 for Kindle. But, I don't like to brag about this, but I was, for a while, the Easter Bunny. I was actually, technically, the backup Easter Bunny.

The day that I got drafted into that, because I was actually working on the First Lady's staff for a short period of time, and I had to go into a restroom to change. As I was changing, two uniformed Secret Service agents came in, and these guys started laughing so hard when I'm standing there in this bunny suit, they literally were rolling on the floor. And just to add to the humiliation, what some of them did after that for a while was they left carrots on my desk.

Then, just to layer one more on top of that, I decided one day, you know, I was a kid. I was doing all those things that anybody without a fully formed frontal lobe does, and I decided that I would cut from the East Wing to the West Wing, but I would do it across what most people would call the front lawn. It was a really bad idea, and I tripped off God knows how many alarms, and all of these uniformed Secret Service agents come running over and one of them points and looks and he goes, "Never mind. It's just the Easter Bunny."

Gary: It's the Easter Bunny, yeah.

Donald: So, I had that. I felt privileged to be able to write a book that shares history, but a lot of funny stuff that happened and a lot of funny stuff that I saw.

Gary: Nowadays for someone to, never mind get this job or get to the level that you were within that job and around the people that you were, I think would almost be impossible. So, quite the experience. Quite the life experience. And, again, writing the book. I think it was great, because when I'm reading and I'm thinking to myself, "Boy, this was a very dark time in America." But the humor and the comical things that you put into it kept it in perspective. I mean, we're not going to change history, but it did keep it in perspective and it made one feel like, "Okay, now if I was there, what would I be doing?" But it was quite the trip that you were through in the White House.

Now, were you there the day that President Nixon left?

Donald: Oh, yes. In fact, the night that he spoke to the nation to tell everybody he was going to resign, actually, I helped friends of mine take the furniture out of the Oval Office so they could get the cameras in. Because in those days, those were huge cameras.

Gary: Right.

Donald: And in one of the more poignant moments, and you can read about it more. There was a lot of funny stuff that happened around that. There's some very weird, bizarre kinds of things. But in one of the more poignant moments, at least for me, I was standing not that far away from then Vice-President and Mrs. Ford, as President Nixon stood giving that famous wave from the helicopter. I noticed something, and what I noticed was that the football, the bag with nuclear codes had stayed behind with him, because under the 25th Amendment, he would become president the moment Nixon's resignation took effect.

Gary: So, Donald, again. How can people find you and get your book?

Donald: You can go to: downstairsatthewhitehouse.com. The book is available on Amazon, barnesandnoble.com. We're in several presidential libraries, and I hope everybody has the chance to enjoy it.

Gary: Donald, thanks for joining us this morning. Great book. I'm glad you sent me a copy of it, and it was great having you on.

Donald: Gary, you're a great guy. Thank you so much for having me. I really appreciate it. Have a great day.

Gary: You're welcome.

11

CYNTHIA GARRETT

Gary:　　　Anyone who has a child in college, nephew, grandson, a friend who has a child in college, who wants to listen to our next guest in the next segment. We have attorney Cynthia Garrett on the line with us.

Cynthia is the co-president of Families Advocating for Campus Equality. FACE. And the board president of Stop Abusive and Violent Environments, SAVE. Cynthia, welcome to the show.

Cynthia:　　Thank you for having me.

Gary:　　　It's my pleasure. So, the president the other day made some tweets. We know how the president tweets, and some people like it, some people don't. But on this one, I thought he is right on target. Having watched this particular topic for a number of years now, when he said, "What happened to due process?"

Even some of the other things he's said, Cynthia, in the last 48 hours he tweeted, "People's lives have been shattered and destroyed by mere allegation. There is no recovery for someone who's falsely accused. Life and career are gone." And there's no such thing any longer of due process.

And I think, when it comes to this subject matter, I think the president was right on with this

Cynthia:　　I agree with you completely. I think due process is being whittled away every year, and it started years ago with radical feminist ideology, about this being a patriarchy that most of America ignored, slowly has infiltrated the colleges and of course, they graduated all those Women's Studies majors who are now causing even law enforcement to start by believing.

And that's actually the name of the campaign.

Gary: Yes, it is.

Cynthia: Start by Believing.

Gary: And I want to get into that. But, as you know, it's somewhat become somewhat taboo to ask for due process before determining someone's guilt. It's absolutely insane. And this guilty until proven innocent has become the norm. And on college campuses, there are individuals who have been charged with crimes, rape, that are just pure allegations.

Lives have been ruined. Families have been ruined. Lives have been taken. Suicide. The individual's accused family members. And it's become a horrific thing. No one is purporting that, if someone committed the crime, that they shouldn't be investigated and let due process take its course.

But this jump to "you're guilty" before there's been any investigation is a very scary way to go.

Cynthia: You're absolutely right, and at FACE we have hundreds of families that have come to us as a result of the college systems. And most of them can't get into another college. They're so traumatized that they have. A lot of our parents, the first time they get a call, it's from the hospital because the kid tried to commit suicide.

Gary: Right.

Cynthia: So, I completely agree with you. Their lives, they're despondent. They have PTSD. They are so traumatized. Some can't even talk to a girl anymore. And these are kids that are innocent. And we know they're innocent, because we know their stories. And all the stories are very similar to each other.

The guy breaks up with the girl, she's mad, and she sees him with another girl. Her boyfriend finds out she had sex. He needs an excuse for exams. Same stories. Over & over.

Gary: Let me ask you this. Why is the due process right under such attack on college campuses? Or in general?

Cynthia: According to the Obama administration, they specifically informed colleges that they were not to allow due process to interfere with the rights of a complainant. So, colleges took that message and created these procedures that don't allow the student to see the accusation against them. They don't even let them know specifically what they're accused of.

They won't let them see the evidence. They won't let them have an attorney who can actually speak. It goes on and on. No cross-examination. And that all came down from the Obama administration.

Which is why Betsy DeVos rescinded some of that guidance. Because she wants schools to pay more attention to both sides of the issue.

And that's what we support. We don't support taking away victims' rights or protections which all these victims' advocates are now complaining about. We support rights for victims, but we also support fairness for everybody.

Gary:

Right. And I mean, the mainstream media has a way of flipping that around so it looks like, if it was someone who was legitimately raped or something did happen, that certain groups are trying to cover that up. And that's nowhere near the case.

Becasue I did a lot of reading when I had you coming on, and I'm reading some of these articles. And shame, shame on them for bringing out that, purporting to make that an issue. Because we all know that's not the case. People just want justice. If you're innocent, you're innocent.

So, those that accuse someone of sexual assault, why are they treated different in our court systems?

Cynthia:

Why are the school teachers treated differently? Because of Title IX. Because apparently they consider it discrimination.

It started back in the 70s with Title IX, and that was all about athletics. And all of a sudden, and I can't remember the exact time sequence, but all of a sudden, discrimination included sexual harassment. Okay, fine. If it's a teacher harassing a student, I see that because there's a power differential.

And then, all of a sudden, this sexual harassment included sexual assault. And the whole power differential issue got thrown out the window. So it started applying to students upon student harassment and assault.

And the Obama administration told the colleges to lower their standard of evidence to more likely than not. So basically it's a wave.

The problem with that was, the Office of Civil Rights of the Department of Education was very punitive towards the colleges enforcing this. They would put the college's name on a list publicly, if they simply got one complaint from some complainants whose case wasn't treated fairly. They didn't even investigate it before they put the colleges on the list.

So, as a result, colleges were terrified, and they tried to do everything they could in order to not have OCR, that's how we say Office of Civil Rights, on their backs.

Gary: At whatever cost it was to an individual or family, and that's what we're starting to see. When I read some of these stories, Cynthia, and you see, as we talked about it a little bit, what happens to students. Whether they have to leave the college, or they can't get to another school, or their lives spin out of control.

But also, the family. The family is traumatized by this. There's a financial burden on the family. And I was reading some cases where parents who had other kids that should have been going to college were not going to go to at least college where they had the opportunity to stay over, they were so affected by this. Their lives were ruined.

Cynthia: We've had people lose homes. We had a family spend over a million dollars. It's really tragic. And you know the reason, especially that's tragic is, the kids that are really getting affected by this are the minorities and lower-income students who don't have the money to hire a lawyer.

Because once you hire a lawyer, at least the school tries to pay more attention. It doesn't always work, but it works more than if you didn't have an attorney.

Gary: Exactly. And then, when you look at what the schools or the policing process now, and I love some of the stuff that you say. With police investigators believing that someone if they were saying they were raped, just believing it. That's the end of it.

That's the way they're taking the investigation. Where, we all hope that law enforcement is going to talk to both parties and try to come up with the truth based on the information that they gain.

Cynthia: You're right about that, too. I mean, I can see believing someone who says they were raped if you're a counselor. Or even an interviewer. Because that does elicit more information if there actually was a rape.

But, to pass it on to the investigator, who has an ethical obligation to be objective and investigate both sides, and tell an investigator that he or she must start by believing. And then, on top of that, we have all these neurobiology theories, and I say theories because I don't believe they've been proven, that complainants, oh, they give inconsistent statements, and that's a result of trauma.

Or they behave inconsistently. For example, we have a lot of cases where, this girl and the young man dated for months after the supposed assault, but then, after they break up there's a complaint. The student, of course, says, "Well, wait a minute! She slept with me for another six months!"

That's not relevant, because it's counter-intuitive behavior. And victims exhibit counter-intuitive behaviors. So there's no way to defend yourself.

Gary: No. It's crazy. You're listening to Cynthia Garrett. My name is Gary. We're going to take a short break, and we'll be right back to Business, Politics and Lifestyles.

On the line with me is attorney Cynthia Garrett. Attorney Garrett is co-president at Families Advocating for Campus Equality, FACE, and board president of Stop Abusive and Violent Environments, SAVE.

Believe the victim investigations, and trauma-informed police training. First of all, I have to wonder. How did this develop? How did this start?

Because when I look at the map, and we'll give out your websites at the end when you show that map of the states, four states are using this. A lot of them have legislation where they're trying to enact this type of investigation. It just doesn't seem like they have their hands on the right pulse here.

Cynthia: No, it doesn't. It started, like I said earlier, back with this radical feminist ideology that believes America's patriarchy, and then, in the '90s colleges started to start by believing. They would chant that. Start by believing. Start by believing, because they were worried about victims.

So I think part of the attitude is, that these advocates believe that this is somehow a solution that's supposed to make up for past wrongs. And in the past, those who've complained about being assaulted have been ignored. I don't think anybody doubts that.

But today, the special victim's units are entirely different than they were 20, 30 years ago. I think they're much more sensitive to the issues of someone who's been raped.

And then, it developed into colleges, and here we are, and all of a sudden it's going into the criminal justice system. Which honestly, I find frightening. Because it does upend our whole system of presumption of innocence.

Gary: Right. I mean, it's like putting a finger on the scale and weighing it to one side over the other, and that's a scary thing. You talk to parents all the time. Probably who have kids that are being faced with charges or something to that nature.

We know how and we've talked about how traumatic it is. What do you usually have to do? What is the process you go through with them to try to help them out?

Cynthia: Well, they have a huge emotional need. Every one of those hundreds of families calls it a nightmare. The worst thing they've ever experienced. We have people. One woman who said her husband died of brain cancer. Horrendous. And her experience with her son going through this process was worse.

So you can imagine, we need to give them emotional support, and we try to have events where they can get together and talk to each other. We try to connect them with people in their area, or similar schools. And the emotional support they even give each other is enormous.

Because the people who have already been through this, help the new people come forward.

That's our primary mission. But we also do advocacy. And we go to DC and we try to talk to congressmen, and that kind of thing. But we recommend, if they can afford it, that families hire lawyers. And we do try to provide pro bono cases, but we can only do that in such a few cases because we are not a well-funded organization.

In fact, one of our necessities over the next six months is to begin serious fundraising. Because we need to help these people. A lot of them can't even afford to come to the meetings that we have.

And so, we try to get scholarships for people to be able to attend. Especially students. Because you don't want to tell anybody what's happened. Whether you're a parent or student, you're embarrassed. They're going to think you did something wrong.

And the only people that understand are the people that have been through this crazy, mixed-up college system.

Gary: Yeah. And you know, which brings me to my point that even when you read the horror stories of when these individuals, you know, it's proven that they're innocent, that guilt somehow lingers on with them.

People say, "Yeah, they're innocent, but..." There's always that "but", and to go through life with that "but," or even thinking that you're going through life with that "but" is very difficult.

Cynthia: It's a big "but."

Gary: It is.

Cynthia: I mean, if you look at some of the cases that are 20, 30 years old and I don't remember his name, but there was a young man who'd been accused at some college in the Northeast, and he'd been found not responsible.

And yet, he tried to produce a movie a year or two ago, and all of a sudden all of these allegations came out, and hurt his career seriously.

The Duke lacrosse kids still can't work. It still follows them. People still think they're guilty.

The young man at Columbia who Emma Sulkowicz or mattress girl you know traumatized, was found not responsible twice by the school on a very low standard of evidence. And yet, she has ruined his life.

Gary: Yeah. And that's the part that, when you read some of the stories online, and you read what's happened to these individuals, you're talking first of all, like you said earlier, sometimes the kids don't even see this coming. It blindsides them.

But then, you're talking about individuals that have gone to schools that had potential to really do some great things, whose lives have just been devastated. It's absolutely crazy.

I want to give people your website at the end of the show, because when you go through your website and you look at some of the things that you have on there, but even you have this Ten Myths of Campus Sexual Assault, I found through your website, and you read through some of that stuff.

And I'm saying to myself, we're led to believe by the way things are reported to us that some of these facts are true just by the way someone reads it to you on a news cast, or when in fact, a lot of times, they're just giving you a little of the narrative that isn't really what it's meant out to be.

Cynthia: Yeah. If every time I hear one in five women are assaulted on campus, or one in four, it makes me crazy. Because those studies are based on very broad definitions. Did you have sex while intoxicated? Well, on college, that happens all the time.

Did someone touch you when you felt you didn't want them to touch you in some sexual way? It goes on and on. And also, the thing that's even worse is, a lot of times they ask these people that are taking the survey questions. Specific questions. Did this happen to you? And they don't ask them if they've been assaulted.

And yet, the authors of the studies will characterize them as victims based on the questions, and yet, when they ask them why they didn't report they said, "Well, I felt I was personally responsible." A huge percentage say that.

Or, it didn't seem that big of a deal. So you see how these figures are being inflated by these studies.

Gary: Yeah. Yeah. It's sad. And as we're getting to the bottom of the hour, I do want to talk to you about your Campus Equality Fairness and Transparency Act at SAVE. Did you want to talk about that?

Cynthia: We put it together to try to balance the interest of both parties. To provide basic due process. Let kids see the evidence against them. Give them somebody that can help with them. I mean, these are normally freshmen and sophomores. Young kids. They get this email saying they've been accused, and they think, "Well, I didn't do anything wrong, so I'll just go in and tell them what happened."

And they believe that that school is going to be fair. They believe that that school is going to hear their side of the story and understand what the truth is. But that's not what happens. So they go into these hearings, and they're blindsided.

Gary: Right.

Cynthia: "I'm guilty?" You know why.

Gary: I just don't think they grasp the severity of what the situation at hand is, either.

Cynthia: Of course.

Gary: We've had children, or nieces and nephews in college. You know how they are, especially freshman and sophomore year. And then all of a sudden, they're in the world of real life here.

                If you could give some advice to a parent whose kids are either in school or going off to school, is there any one thing you'd have to say to them?

Cynthia: Don't have sex with a girl who's intoxicated. That sounds harsh, but I have to tell you that later they'll say, "I was too intoxicated to give consent." Not incapacitated. A lot of the schools just say intoxicated.

Gary: Right.

Cynthia: Be sure that the person you choose to date is emotionally stable.

Gary: Yep.

Cynthia: Because a lot of them are very needy. They have issues. And these young, sweet boys want to help them. We see that all the time.

Gary: Sorry to interrupt you. We're at the bottom of the hour. Do you want to just give out the information where people can find you?

Cynthia: Yes. facecampusequality.org, or if you need help with support and emotional and advice as far as attorneys, and saveservices.org if you want to get involved with the legislative end.

Gary: Since it was great having you on, I definitely want to have you back on and talk about this topic in a little more detail. Thank you for coming on today.

Cynthia: I'd love to. Thank you.

12

BRIGITTE GABRIEL

Gary:	On the line with me right now is Brigitte. Brigitte has been named one of the top 50 most prominent speakers in America. She is a New York Times bestselling author, a leading expert on global Islamic terrorism, and chairman of Act! For America, the largest national security grassroots organization in America. She is the author of the books, Because They Hate a Survivor of Islamic: Terror Warns America, and They Must Be Stopped: Why we Must Defeat Radical Islam and How We Can Do It Now, and her new book which will be out, I believe on 9/11, it's called Rise.

Good Morning, Brigitte. Welcome to the show.

Brigitte: Good Morning, Gary. Delighted to be with you.

Gary: So I received your advanced copy of the book last night, and read about a third of it, and I must tell you, the first third has already sent chills up and down my spine. When you read what's, you know, when you read that book. And I want to talk about that a little bit, because in this book, you talked about what's going on in the world today; and America could be affected by terrorism. I have so many friends of mine that believe that since 9/11, we've been pretty much safe and nothing can happen again. My theory is, Brigitte, that everything comes in waves and I hate to be pessimistic but it's a matter of time if we don't defend ourselves properly.

Brigitte: You know, in America, we have a very short attention span. I mean, the terrorism issue was not even on the radar screen of anybody until last week when we found out that a radical Islamist has a compound in New Mexico and he is training 10 children to go shoot schools. You would expect to hear a story like this coming out of the Palestinian territory. You would expect a story like this coming out of Gaza where a radical Islamic man training kids to infiltrate or run towards Israelis and start shooting or killing school children.

But to hear that being done in America, all of a sudden, brought back the issue of radicalism, radical Islamic terrorism to the forefront. We're not out of the woods just because President Trump has successfully defeated the ISIS and ended their physical caliphate does not mean that ISIS is no longer a threat.

The caliphate is right now on the Internet, their videos, their YouTubes, their magazines. And not only ISIS. You've got Hezbollah, you've got Al Qaeda, you've got other terrorist organizations with their own very same famous figures, with their own YouTube videos on the Internet where young children or young adults, young and old actually, who are drawn into that type of radicalism, are still up and operating just because we're not seeing them and we're not hearing them; and thank God we were able to stop this man in New Mexico and arrest him and save these poor kids, and find out what was happening.

I mean, if they were to pull that off, then we would be having a completely different conversation right now.

Gary: We'd have a completely much different conversation and what's even scarier that I read recently is some of those that were arrested have been released on bail, which is-

Brigitte: Exactly.

Gary: Absolutely, Brigitte, these are the types of things that just make me crazy. I can't even fathom how a judge could let somebody out like this.

Brigitte: Exactly. I mean, and let them out on bail. Think about this, Gary. This story has so many levels, so many levels. You've got a radical Islamist operating this scam. He has 10 children that he is starving them. They are living in a really bad situation. One child found dead. By the way, that was his son which the father had killed in an Islamic religious ritual. Then he had three wives that he was married to. One of them was illegally in the country for 20 years.

The multiple layers to this story. You've got illegal immigration; you've got the multiple marriages; you've got the father abusing his own child and killing his own child. You've got the training kids to shoot schools. I mean, look, we talked about the school shooting in Florida. For how many weeks, people talked about it and organized against guns, this, that and the other just because a guy tragically succeeded in carrying out the attack.

Can you imagine if 10 kids went in to 10 different schools across the country and did that? And on top of that, killing his own child? I remember back about 20 something years ago, there was a woman that killed her two sons. I think her name was Susan something.

Gary: Yeah, I remember that.

Brigitte: Remember that story? She killed her two sons, drowned them in the car.

Gary: Right, she drove the car into the water, right.

Brigitte: That's right. That story was on the media for a month. Every single night, we heard about it. Right now, a father kills his son, you know, chops him up, buries him dead, buries his bones, starves the other 10, it's like talking about the weather. Nobody really cares. Why? Because he is a radical Muslim. Because he's an Islamist, we're not allowed to talk about it.

Gary: Right. We're never going to get the story out of the mainstream media, but thank God for people like yourself, Brigitte. Illegal immigration, resettlement of refugees, how is that hurting our country from your perspective. I have friends that when I talk to them about this think I'm racist, I'm mean-spirited, and when you try to have an intelligent conversation, never mind from the safety point of view, diseases or whatever, they don't want to talk about it, Brigitte.

Brigitte: Exactly. Here's the problem. We now are bringing refugees into this country from third world countries. We are not vetting them. Under Obama, he put them basically on the federal express lanes trying to get them into the United States as fast as he can. I remember when the Syrian refugee's crisis was happening and they fled to Jordan. They had camps in Jordan for these refugees. What Obama did to expedite the refugees being transported to the United States, he sends our supposedly vetters in to Jordan, a country who cannot wait to get rid of these refugees and send them over to America, to expedite the process. So, there's no proper vetting.

But when you look at what these refugees are bringing with them, we now have a crisis in our country with the diseases that they are bringing. We have seen a surge in dangerous diseases like dengue fever, leprosy, malaria, HIV, Aids, tuberculosis, rubella, syphilis, typhus, whooping cough, and many others. Measles was up more than 450% between 2014 and 2015. Hepatitis B was up 300% over three years; and tuberculosis was up 30%.

Right now, tuberculosis is exploding in 16 states across the United States. The state of Wisconsin alone has 118 cases of tuberculosis, and most of them are drug resistant, which means it takes six to eight months to treat a patient, and it costs about 160,000 dollars per patient to be treated.

The four most populous states in America, California, Florida, New York, and Texas accounted for more than half the tuberculosis cases for the entire country with more than 500 cases in each. This is a problem. This is exactly why we need to control who's coming into our country, who they are, what's their background, what diseases they are bringing with them.

I mean, even other than the terrorist threat, just look from the disease factor and what they're bringing to the country. That's a problem.

Gary:

Yeah, and when you speak to people about the diseases, they look at you like your crazy Because nobody does any research. If they don't hear it on the news, the mainstream media, they don't think it exists. But when you research or we listen to someone like yourself and you realize what's going on, the economic cost to this country from the diseases alone is staggering. Taking care of those that are here illegally with the disease and how they spread it to other people, and just the cost of resolving it, it's absolutely crazy.

Brigitte:

Exactly. Gary, you mentioned about it spreading to others; but people who have tuberculosis can walk around for a month infecting other people and nobody else knows. To give you an example, this is why I go into all this detail in my book Rise when I talk about the immigration and replacement civilization and what is that doing to our country. In 2015, 27 students tested positive for tuberculosis at one high school in Kansas City, Kansas alone. That's how contagious tuberculosis is, particularly for children without fully developed immunities.

Now, people don't care about these things until it's your child that is at that school or your grandchild. And then all of a sudden, you're thinking, "Oh my God, there is such an explosion of tuberculosis. Why didn't anybody let me know?" Well, because it's not politically correct to talk about these things. Because it is the refugees and the illegal immigrants who are bringing these types of diseases with them.

But that's exactly why I titled my book Rise. Rise, because right now, Gary, we need Americans to know what to do about the problem and exactly what's happening in the country. To give you an example also about how we are lowering our standards to accommodate these people we are bringing from third world country, as an example, the city of Denver in May 2017, passed an ordinance that allowed people to defecate on sidewalks and the streets and it is no longer a crime. Why? Because Denver is accepting a lot of refugees. It actually has the largest refugee population than San Francisco and Philadelphia.

Because if a police officer stops you or arrests you because you defecated on the sidewalk, then they can deport you. So because of that, the city of Denver decided, "Well, you know what? We need to lower our standards and adopt the standards of people from Mogadishu because after all, don't you all want to be like people from Mogadishu or Somalia? So, it's okay to defecate on the street walks, on the sidewalks. That's not a big deal. Let's just lower our standards and accommodate them."

This is exactly why I titled my book Rise: In Defense of Judeo-Christian Values and Freedom. Because our values, our standards are high standards; and those who are coming into our country, we want them to assimilate to us and raise their standards. We don't want to bring our standard, our standards down to assimilate and adapt to their third world culture.

Gary: No. And much too often, as you said, because of political correctness, that is what happens. I just read an article in San Francisco of how they have crews that help you go up and down the streets to clean these messes up on a daily basis. Who would have thought in America this would ever be an issue, people defecating on the streets as a way of life, Brigitte?

Brigitte: Exactly. You know what, Gary? People like us sat on the sidelines-

Gary: I agree.

Brigitte: ... and shook their heads and think, "Oh my God, I cannot believe how these crazies, how these lefties run these cities". But boy, oh boy, I'm going to vote when election happens". Well, you know what? There's a lot of things that can happen in two years between voting. This is exactly why our side needs to be engaged. It's not only important to know about what's happening. It's important to know what to do about what's happening.

This is what I lay out, as you notice. You're reading my book and my book, Rise, at the end of every chapter, no matter what I'm talking about, whether I'm talking about the death of free speech, I have a chapter titled The Death of Free Speech. Whether I'm talking about operation indoctrination, talking about what's happening in our schools, how they are brainwashing our students, whether I'm talking about immigration or replacement civilization, or the leftist Islamist coalition. Whatever chapter I have in the book, at the end, I have a section titled Rise Up and Act where I give people the things they can do to make a difference for the country.

Not only be informed, but know what to do about the information you are getting and how you can be an instrument of change for the country.

Gary: We're speaking with author Brigitte Gabriel. We're going to take a quick break and bring her back. I just want to talk to her about the TSA and another couple other issues.

We're speaking with author, Brigitte Gabriel. We're talking about her new book Rise.

You know, Brigitte, in your book, you sort of force us to start reacting, not sitting back and waiting. If we want to preserve the values we were brought up on, it's up to us to preserve those values. No one else is going to do it for us.

Brigitte: Exactly. Exactly. You know, it doesn't take many to change the world. It takes only a dedicated few. I always say two percent of the passionate will always rule the 98% indifferent. Two percent. Right now, what we are seeing in our country, Gary, is the left, the radicals are organized. The thugs breaking and killing or destroying property, the Black Lives Matters killing our police, calling them pigs in a blanket.

When you see what's happening in our country, the left is very organized but they do not know anything about the issues. You stop any 22-year-old nitwit and ask them, "Tell me about socialism. Why are you for socialism?" They cannot even answer you what socialism is, but they go out and they block bridges and they stop highways, et cetera.

On our side, you have the educated ones, like obviously every single person listening to this broadcast right now is highly educated and informed about the issues. That's exactly why they listen to you, Gary, and the information you give them and the speakers you have on your show.

It's not that our side lacks information. What our side lacks is what do I do with the information? Give me something to do. A lot of people do not want to worry about, you know... Give me something to do. Tell me what I need to do and I can do it. I just do not want to think about it.

That's what I give them in Rise. We need to rise up in defense of our country because we can no longer shake our head and think, "Oh my goodness, I cannot believe this is happening. I think I'm going to get together with my friends and we're going to hold a meeting and we're going to sit around and discuss how bad the situation is in our country."

Those days are over. We are way past that right now. Right now, we want people to know what they can do, how timely they can do it. I also encourage people to go to our website. You know, I am the founder of actforamerica.org. Actforamerica.org. We are the largest national security grassroots organization in the United States with one million members. We have helped pass 100 bills on the federal level as well as the state level, all relating to national security.

Go to our website actforamerica.org, sign up to get our emails and action alerts, and check out the legislations that we have. Our high priority legislations. Sign up as an activist. You can also there order my book Rise. It will take you directly to Amazon. We need every single person engaged and involved.

Gary: You know, I was sort of giggling when you were talking about socialism. When I talk to younger people about socialism or they talk to me about it, no, no, you've got it wrong. Now, it's democratic socialism. Because they throw democratic in front of it, they think they're changing the tune of socialism. It's funny but it's not funny, Brigitte. It's kind of sad. It's just a scary thought process.

You talk about how we have to educate ourselves and identify behaviors, or if we see things and threat in the community, which I agree with; but too often, people are still afraid. People listening to the show may be afraid to do that because if they do that and it's not a situation, right away, they're afraid to be labeled racists or could it affect my job? We have to get over that fear, Brigitte.

Brigitte: Look, if they're afraid and they do not want to be labeled racists, that's fine. Email us. Get involved with us behind the scenes. I'm the one who's giving radio interviews. We need people supporting us. For example, I'm speaking right now. You do not know the names of the one million members we have. You do not know who they are, where they live. But boy, oh boy, we do know their names and we know how to send them bills coming down for a vote in Congress.

For example, I'm going to share with you a bill that I'm going to ask you, and I know that you are very well informed, Gary. I want to ask if you've heard about it. Have you heard about the bill going through Congress called Protect and Serve Act?

Gary: Yes.

Brigitte: Okay, great, but see, you're very informed. A lot of people have not. It would make police a protected class and violence against them a hate crime. We worked with Congress on that bill; we were able to pass it through the House, and now it is going through the Senate. It's at the Senate Hearing Committee, getting ready to go out of that Committee.

We are urging our members to call the Senate and tell them to move through this bill because we want to make sure that hurting a police officer or killing a police officer is a crime punishable, serving time in prison. Up to life in prison if you kill law enforcement personnel.

This is why we want people informed and engaged about the issue. Plus, you know, I remember the New York Times writing an article about me in 2008 after I wrote my second book. The title of the article, they labeled me not just an Islamophobe, but a radical Islamophobe. Since they labeled me a radical Islamophobe, my organization has now passed 100 bills. 13 bills on the federal level, and over 85 bills on the state level.

If I would have allowed the New York Times to silence me or shame me to sit on the sidelines, 100 bills will not now be, has been as anchored in different states as well as in the federal government to protect our country.

My philosophy is this: if you have to stop and answer every barking dog, you will never reach your destination. So, it doesn't matter what people call you. After they call you Islamophobe, or a racist, or a bigot, or whatever they want to call you, and then what? Then you are free to do whatever you want to do to change the country; and they run out of things to call you or talk to you about because they cannot debate you on ideas. That's why they call you names. They cannot debate your facts. That's why they resort to name-calling. So they let them call you a name and you move on passing bills. At the end of the day, that's what matters.

Gary: You know, you have to go with your own personal moral compass is and believe in what you believe in. If you let other people change and define you, we wouldn't have respect. We'd just be stuck spinning our wheels all the time. We're getting to the bottom of the hour. I do have to ask you one question. Would you call the TSA one of the greatest American failures?

Brigitte: It is the greatest American failure. That's such an important fat chapter in my book. That's an important thing, and I'm going to squeeze in the sentence that I am sure that struck you. But TSA has 95% failure rate. Now, we established that in the chapter. Do you know that we spent over 2.1 billion dollars from 2008 through 2017 on these scanners that the TSA said would provide the most effective and least intrusive way to check travelers for weapons? Those ones you go through, you stand there, you put your hands over your head?

The TSA is now using 793 useless full body scanners funded by you and me at 157 airports as a part of their continued "we've got you covered" theater. But if you tape a gun to the side of your leg, and walk through these scanners, you can literally walk through with undetected because these scanners cannot detect a gun if you place it on the side of your leg. This is how miserable and a failure the TSA is.

When a blogger posted a video of himself walking through one of those TSAs with a gun taped to his leg and going undetected, two million people watched his video on YouTube. TSA felt so embarrassed. One of the supervisors told their employees, they said, "Well, you've got to pat every fifth passenger. Pat them down, pull them away to pat them down so we can show the American public that there are other ways to detect explosives other than these machines".

It's a total waste of money. It's an embarrassment to our nation. It's an embarrassment to our intelligence, Gary. We, the American public, are herded like cattle through the airports, standing in line, taking our shoes off, our belts off, putting our hands over our heads. The reason why we have been so lucky not to have another airline disaster, not because we have been so smart in stopping the idiots. It's because we're dealing with the stupid terrorists who are thankfully stupid enough to actually pull something like this off.

Gary: You're right. Brigitte, that part of your book just struck me. It was like incredible information. Why don't you let people once again know how to get a hold of you and where they can buy your book?

Brigitte: The book is now available on Amazon. The book is titled Rise. Rise by Brigitte Gabriel. You can also get the book by going to our website actforamerica.org. Actforamerica.org. and please get it and share it with every friend you have. The information I have in this book is explosive and it will light a fire under you and every one you know who loves this country and wants to defend our Judeo-Christian values and freedom.

Gary: Brigitte, thank you for joining me this morning. It's been a pleasure and I really do enjoy your book.

Brigitte: Thank you very much. Have a great weekend.

13

EDDIE DOMINGUEZ

Gary: On the line with us now is Eddie Dominguez. He's the author of Baseball Cop, The Dark Side of America's National Pastime. He's a former member of the Major League Baseball's Department of Investigation. Eddie, good morning, and welcome to the show.

Eddie: Good morning, Gary. Thank you for having me on.

Gary: My pleasure. Let's talk a little bit about before you got involved with Major League Baseball. You were a Boston police officer, a Boston detective?

Eddie: That's right, Gary. I came on the job in 1979 and remained on the job until 2008, when I retired.

Gary: Then you went to work for the Red Sox for a bit, was that it?

Eddie: Yeah, I worked in the security department. In 1999, while still a Boston police detective, I was assigned to an FBI drug unit. There, I was approached by the SAC, the special agent in charge of the office in Boston, and asked if I'd be interested in joining Major League Baseball on a part time basis as a resident security agent.

Eddie: What that is is each team in Major League Baseball has an active police officer that acts as the eyes and ears of the commissioner's office in the particular city or town where the actual stadium is located. Obviously, Fenway Park is located in Boston, so it would have been a, it still is a Boston police officer that is the resident security agent.

I interviewed with about 40 other Boston or state police officers, and I was fortunate enough to get the job. That started me on track with baseball in 1999, where I stayed as a resident security agent till 2008, when then I joined full time in the New York office, the commissioner's office in the Department of Investigations.

Gary: In your book, which is a very incredible book. I'm going to preface, I'm not a big baseball guy. It's not my first sport, but reading some of the things that you brought out really opens your eyes. Let's talk about that, when you were first with the Red Sox, some of the things that you saw there that that concerned you, that opened your eyes to there's something maybe going on in Major League Baseball.

Eddie: Yeah, Gary. I joined baseball as a resident security agent thinking, still being a police officer, that as a police officer, you see things, you see crimes, you report them, or you take action and you arrest people, you summon them into court, you follow up on investigations to see whatever it is that brought to your attention, the act that was occurring, if it is a crime.

Eddie: I found, early on, that I was reporting things back to the commissioner's office, to the head of the security, and the way that they were dealing with these issues, to me, wasn't the way that they should be dealt with. Most of them were just swept under the rug.

Gary: Give us an example of an issue, if you could.

Eddie: Yeah. There was numerous. In the book Baseball Cop, I bring them out. One of them was, and it got a lot of play here in Boston, but I didn't mean it to, I was just trying to show that this is the way that the security department handled things, but it concerned David Ortiz and his right hand guy, a guy by the name of Monga. He was referred to as Monga.

I had sources in the Dominican community. I worked narcotics most of the time, and this individual, Monga, just didn't look right from the moment I saw him. I found out what the name he was using, that he was going by, I did a little research, and I found out that he had assumed that name, that it wasn't his name. Obviously, that, right away, caused me concern. Why would somebody take on somebody else's name if he wasn't involved in anything?

I had a couple of my informants look into him to see what he was doing. I found out that he and David were visiting a barbershop on Blue Hill Avenue. This barbershop was not only a barber shop, it was a betting parlor as well. My informant told me then, on one specific day, this individual, who by the way didn't have a job, all he did was take care of David, his kids, and drove him around, and he put a bet on the Chicago White Sox to beat the Boston Red Sox, as well as he took the over in the game. He bet what they call an action reverse, and he hit on both ends of it. The White Sox beat the Red Sox, and I believe the score, he had to over with eight runs, and they did.

Eddie: This caused concern, because baseball comes across as being a sport that watches out so that the players aren't betting on baseball, Pete Rose being the example that they use over and over again. So I informed the head of the security about this. I also took action as a police officer, and not only investigated this particular barbershop, but numerous others across Massachusetts, and opened up an investigation. It wasn't up to me to investigate Ortiz. I looked more for his friend Monga. I look more into the actual person that's taken the bet.

We got an investigation on the criminal side, and then I waited for the security side, to see what they were going to do. In my mind, I thought they were going to hire a private investigator and check and see exactly what was going on.

What ended up happening is, one day, unannounced, I get a call by the head of security to pick him up at Logan airport. We drive to Fenway Park, where we meet in Tito Francona's office with David, myself and Kevin Hallinan who was the head of security.

Kevin proceeded to tell David that his friend Monga, that we were watching his friend Monga, and that he was gambling. David denied that that was occurring. We stayed in the stadium for about three innings after that. As we were leaving the stadium, I get a call from my source, who tells me that he had received a call from the barber telling him not to come and place bets at his parlor anymore, because he had been tipped that it was being watched by the police.

Gary: Yeah. Ortiz, David seemed to take this personally. You never made accusations against him, correct?

Eddie: No, no. In the book I had no information that David himself was gambling. I say that in Baseball Cop, but I do say that I didn't think that the investigation was handled the proper way. I would've thought they would've looked into it deeper and tried to find out exactly where Monga got his money to place such a large bet, seeing that he didn't have a job.

Gary: Yeah, and betting, as we know from the Pete Rose incident, that's a no no, and it should be a no no. What ever happened to Monga?

Eddie: Monga, we opened up a criminal investigation on Monga. I turned over the information that I had to ICE agents who were able to find out that Monga had assumed two or three different names along the way. One of the names that he assumed was a Puerto Rican male's name. He had purchased his Social Security, birth certificate. Unknown to him was that this Puerto Rican male was actually wanted for trafficking cocaine back in Puerto Rico. Amongst other things, they found out that Monga paid an American female to marry him, just to gain residency in the United States. He was tried and deported soon thereafter by the federal ICE agents.

Gary: When I knew you were coming on, read the book, and then I went online and Googled articles. I was a little bit shocked at some of the comments Ortiz made about you and your book, which I thought was personally out of place. This was just a means to sell books, but everything you did was legal. It's not like you were out as a private investigator. You were working for an authority. You had reporting relationships, and you were following what you had to do.

Eddie: Yeah, that's right, Gary. I didn't write this book to make money, Gary. I wrote this book because I'm a great fan of sports in general. You said you're not a fan of baseball. I'm a fan of all sports.

I tried them all. I wasn't very good at any of them, but my kids all play sports. I think sports is a good way to bring up your kids. I think it teaches you, it should teach you respect. It should teach you how to win, and more importantly, how to lose in a proper manner. It should teach you that it should be an even playing field, and that's not what I saw when I joined Major League Baseball.

I think a lot of people, like myself, before I joined baseball, think of it differently, think of it as a wholesome, tight sport. In reality, the business side of it is very ugly. I bring that out in Baseball Cop. Not only do I bring it out as far as the commissioner's office, but the individual teams, the international incidents that are going on in baseball, which recently got some news in Sports Illustrated about an ongoing FBI grand jury that's looking into human trafficking, and the stealing of money from young, very poor Latin American players.

I wrote it to bring this out, to give people a look behind the scenes as to what goes on in this multibillion-dollar industry that we call America's Pastime. As far as the money goes, if you read the book, you know that I'm donating half of whatever I get to pancreatic cancer research, something that's very dear to me.

Gary: We're talking with Eddie Dominguez, author of the book Baseball Cop. We're going to take a short break. My name is Gary Goldman. You're listening to Business, Politics and Lifestyles.

On the line with me now is Eddie Dominguez. He's the author of Baseball Cop. Eddie, how long was that stay of yours with the police department and the Red Sox? When you were with the police department in Boston, was that actually part of the Major League job that you took, or that was separate, wasn't it, when you were just with the Red Sox?

Eddie: Yeah. I was a resident security agent. I was a contract employee. Like I said, I interviewed for that job, and then on a yearly basis I had gained permission from the Boston police commissioner to allow me to take part in this job. You did it on your own time, like doing a detail in a construction site or something like that.

Eddie: It just happened that I was working for the Red Sox, not for the Red Sox, for the Baseball Commissioner's office, but I'm a Boston cop, I'm assigned to Fenway Park. What that entailed was helping with anything that the security department at Fenway had issues with, giving them another set of eyes and ears to help them with anything that I saw that was going bad in the stadium. Then you assist them with security, the security of the players and the front office people. One of the things that I did was travel with them to Yankee Stadium between 1999 and 2004, because at that time they didn't really have a head of security, so I acted somewhat like that, especially when they traveled abroad. In 2004, they hired a full time head of security, so I stepped aside as far as traveling with the team went, but I got to see a lot of interesting things.

Gary: Oh, I'm sure. I'm sure the things you, incredible things. Just what's in the book raises your eyebrows. But when you met, and I want to get onto the other side of this, but when you met with Francona and Ortiz, at that point, what was the team's reaction to all of that? I'm just curious.

Eddie: At that particular time, when we first met, there wasn't much reaction, but soon thereafter, when the federal investigation ended up with the arrest of Monga, I received a phone call from Theo Epstein, and basically the conversation didn't end very well. I think he was a great guy, but I think he was a little confused as to who I was and what my job was. Theo, on the day that Monga was arrested, Monga was arrested at David's house, and David was upset and called Theo, and then Theo was upset. I was actually staking out a drug dealer when I received the phone call from Theo. He was upset because he thought that I worked for him and for the Red Sox, and that, how could I possibly do something like that to David? After listening to him, I asked him if he was done, and he said he was, and I straightened him out. I said, "No. First of all, Theo, I'm a police officer, first and foremost."

Gary: Right, exactly.

Eddie: Yeah. And secondly, I do not work for the Boston Red Sox. I do a part time job for the commissioner's office in baseball, but my job isn't to look the other way when I see a crime. That's not what I was sworn in, in the city of Boston, Boston police officer to do. We had a couple of words. Afterwards, I think he respected what I said to him, and I understand where he was coming from. I just thought he was a bit confused.

Gary: Yeah, and that's the part that just amazes me. I think what some of the things your book points out to me is not just at the Red Sox, but on the League office, they want the appearance, at times, that they're doing the right thing to keep things under control, but they don't want to hear the results of what someone like you may bring back to them.

Eddie: That's right, Gary. On many occasions, as I point out in the book, in different instances where we were working hand in hand with law enforcement, and I think in the book you'll read from DEA agents and FBI agents and federal prosecutors about their thoughts as to how baseball behaved in these investigations, but on more than one occasion, I was told by the commissioner, then Bud Selig and now Rob Manfred, who was his second in command at the time, do they know, as far as us talking to federal agencies, who we are. I used to laugh at that, because yeah, they were very much aware of who you are, but are you aware who they are? These are federal agents doing a criminal investigation, and what you want them to do is not what a federal investigator should do.

Gary: Right, right. First of all, how many people were in this Department of Investigation? How many people like yourself for Major League Baseball?

Eddie: Yeah, just a little background on how Department of Investigations came about. It came about as a result of congressional hearings that were held in 2005 when baseball, for the first time in a long time, had their feet held to the fire, because if you had half a brain, you realized that baseball was looking the other way as far as the use of performance enhancing substances. This is the era where Sammy Sosa and Mark McGuire are hitting balls like if they were golf balls, out the stadium, breaking records that had lasted for decades. There were congressional hearings. There were threats from Congress that they were thinking of taking away some of the benefits that baseball has, and so Bud Selig hired former senator George Mitchell, who did an investigation. In 2007, he came back with a report. In the report, he made recommendations. The report basically confirmed that baseball and the Players Association had, for years, turned a blind eye in the use of PEDs, and other incidents that called into question the integrity of the game.

So our unit was formed. It was going to be separate from the security unit. It should not work with the Labor Department of Major League Baseball because, Senator Mitchell pointed out, that the Labor Department deals with the Players Association for their contract, and so at times they find themselves in situations where, to get a better deal from the Players Association, they will look the other way on incidents that they shouldn't, they should report to the police. So we were supposed to be an autonomous unit made up of law enforcement officials that were respected not only in the local but federal law enforcement. As I said, I had worked with the FBI drug unit and with the DEA.

Myself and two New York police officers were hired as the first investigators. We were under Dan Mullin, who was one of the chiefs of police in New York, and George Hanna, who was the head of the Organized Crime Unit for the FBI in New York. It was five of us at first. We grew. At one point, there was six investigators, and the two chiefs, and a staff of analysts that worked with us. The minute we started investigating, we found out that PEDs weren't the only issues that baseball had. International issues were brought to our attention, and they had been going on for decades, and baseball had been turning a blind eye for decades.

Gary: That didn't surprise you at all, did it?

Eddie: It didn't, from the time that I had spent in the security department.

Gary: Right.

Eddie: By the way, I was asked on two different occasions to join full time in New York, the security department, and I declined both offers. I did so because I didn't want to be part of that. That's not why I joined the Boston Police Department. That's not who I am. I didn't want to look the other way, and so I declined. Then I joined DOI because I was sold on it, because we were supposed to work with law enforcement officials any time that we saw anything. We did, but along the way, Bug Selig and Rob Manfred did away with us.

Gary: Yeah. That's what I was alluding to earlier, when they would hear things, or you'd bring things forward, that they didn't want to deal with, instead of dealing with the issue, they get rid of the people that are there trying to solve the problem for them, which is absolutely absurd, Eddie.

Eddie: I know, Gary. It was very frustrating. As I point out in the book, within the first year, I gave serious thought of just coming back. I had retired early. I was in my early fifties when I joined Department of Investigation. I still had, I believe, good years left to offer to the City of Boston. I thought of coming back, and I was talked out of it by my two bosses, who I still highly respect, so I stayed with them. But yeah, it just got very frustrating. As I point out in the book, incidents that, if tackled at that time, would've solved a lot of the issues that they're going to be facing now with this federal grand jury.

Gary: Right, right. You were the bearer of the news they didn't want to hear. Eddie, as we get to the bottom of the hour, tell people where they can get your book, because it's definitely a great read.

Eddie: Yeah. Thank you. The book was written by two good friends of mine, Teri Thompson and Christian Red. Both used to be investigative sports reporters for the New York Daily News. You can pick it up on Amazon, at Barnes & Noble, all the regular places where you can pick up a book.

Gary: And the proceeds go to…

Eddie: As far as whatever I earn, I can't speak obviously for the publisher, but I speak for myself, they go towards research, pancreatic cancer research. I was diagnosed with it soon after being let go from baseball. Along the way, I've met a lot of other people that were diagnosed as well that are not around anymore. It's a disease that nobody, you can never really tell beforehand that you have it. You're either lucky and something happens where they catch it on time, or by the time they catch it, you have a short period of time to live.

Gary: Well, we'll pray-

Eddie: I'm trying to raise money for research.

Gary: Wow. We'll pray for you on a regular basis. Great book, Eddie. It was great having you here this morning. I appreciate you taking the time.

Eddie: Thank you, Gary.

Gary: Thank you.

14

NADRA ENZI

Gary: Our next guest also known as Cap Black and the Hood Conservative, Project 21 member, Nadra Enzi is an outspoken anti-crime activist based in New Orleans, Louisiana, one of my favorite places. Good morning and welcome to the show.

Nadra Enzi: Greetings fellow hostages.

Gary: Greetings to you. We touched about this topic last week and then I got ahold of your organization and Judy was able to get me, you want to speak with us, but this whole Detroit school board can, trying to change the name of the school that was named after Ben Carson, blacklisting Doctor Carson because his association with the Trump administration. I happened to be a big fan of Ben Carson and I just found this outrageous and you know, look at, people in their minds can think they're going to erase history or erase, you know, certain things, but changing the name to me is just outrageous. This is a guy that's done some really great things and why wouldn't we want to promote amongst young children, a great mind who has done great things.

Nadra Enzi: I wholeheartedly agree. But again, in a city that's number two for murder in America, this was where you find decision makers focusing their energy, I mean that, we can start with just a list of family from the anti intellects, anti-achievement, anti-America. I mean, what you're telling me is that it's all right to grow up in the projects but not achieve, strive the spirits heights, we don't want you to do that because if you associate it with one person, because remember Dr. Carson was loved by the left until he just happened to do one thing, go to a prayer breakfast and speak his mind about certain issues. How dare he? And now he has been demonized by the very people who only mere years ago had him on the map of, you know how in lot of families you would have the pictures on the wall of Dr. King and Kennedy Brothers.

Gary: Right.

Nadra Enzi: You know; Dr. Carson could easily have been the fourth picture.

Gary: I agree.

Nadra Enzi: I mean he was revered by the mainstream of America until he announced that he was the conservative. And this was again the anti-intellectual, anti-achievement orientation that fills jail cells, mental wards, probation and parole offices. But just saying that this man who came from, like the old thing came from so called nothing but no one comes to nothing but someone who came from the most austere environments, and became the number one pediatric neurosurgeon and then for bonus almost became president, And now as a presidential appointee. Has given millions of dollars to help young people pull themselves up by their bootstraps, and then you have a group of idiots, I hate to say it, I'm sorry if I'm being indelicate, but you have a group of idiots who want to take his name off of a school and remove whatever as for race and children in the same position he grew up in half. I, you know as mind boggling as a shame. I would say it's shameful to clearly was a situation where shame was not opposite.

Gary: No. And here's, you know, the school was named after Doctor Carson as you know in 2013. It features a college preparatory curriculum that is devoted to guiding students towards discovering their career potential while visualizing themselves as college graduates. I always thought these are the things we wanted to aspire in our children. We want them to realize their potential and have great role models. Role models to me are very important. And now to just pretend that Doctor Carson is not a role model. I mean someone needs to shut the door behind the school board and have a little conversation with them because this is absolutely absurd. They can shoot, they can, they can reduce the name, they can do what they want. Unfortunately, it's not going to change who Doctor Carson is, but this is just not right on so many different levels in people all over this country need to speak up and show outrage over this.

Nadra Enzi: I absolutely agree and I keep going back to, I grew up in an urban area where there were role models, men like my grandfather. Men like our first black mayor, great man who achieved distinction against odds, much more entrenched than where young people face today. So in Detroit with this myriad problems, you're telling me that the way to make sure young people stop getting involved in gangs, stop going to jail, stop killing each other, is to take Ben Carson's name off of a school in the city that's number two in the nation for murder. It's, you know, it would be comical if it weren't so tragic because this is the anti-intellectual, anti-achievement orientation. They had too many black people who should know better, quite frankly, buy into. Because they are thinking as ideological zealots and not as stewards of the public trust. Again, a man raised by a mother who was illiterate but did not tell him she was illiterate and in turn made him a world class academician and number one in the world. As a neurosurgeon, I was, you know, I'm just going to pause a moment and think, isn't that the type of mindset you would want? Not just the inner city American children, but all American children. No excuses. Go for the Gusto, achieve beyond anybody's wildest dreams. Isn't that what we want? Isn't that what we should have in this country? I think so.

Gary: Yeah.

Nadra Enzi: And I think people should be outraged because it's not a ideological issue. I'd go back to, I haven't used the word conserve, but I did use it once, but this isn't a conservative issue per se, is not a republican issue per se, even though those are definitely at the basis of this. My great concern is what you're telling young people in Detroit and by extension around the country in our inner cities is don't achieve, don't be intellectual only do with a highest mind tells you to do. And if not, then the urban version of the Taliban are gonna come and, and strike your name from the public record.

Gary: Yeah, yeah.

Nadra Enzi: And there's a great message in the greatest country in the world to send our people.

Gary: Yeah. The school board member who told The Washington Post that he thinks Doctor Carson's name is synonymous with having President's Trump name on our school, um, in black face and then the fame, you know, so, so because he works in this administration, we need to take his name off cause it's synonymous with President Trump and he's disgracing himself by being associated with president Trump. I mean, you know what, when I first of all out of, as you said, when you get onto the show this morning, and I think the school board ought to be concerned about securing their school and educating their students as opposed to worrying about this. But it, it is where we are in America today and I think this, this speaks volume and these are the types of problems and our, our, whether it's a board member, whether it's a politician, they're out of touch with reality, with what is really going on around them. But I wonder how they can't see what's really going on around them.

Nadra Enzi: Well to be honest with you, when you suffer from, and I think some of your listeners will get a chuckle out of this, the Trump derangement syndrome.

Gary: Yup.

Nadra Enzi: Anyone associated with him is fair game to villainize because at the end of the day, his opponents and again project 21 is a nonpartisan organization.

Gary: Right, great organization. Yeah.

Nadra Enzi: Yeah, I'm just giving you an observation. His opponents are still having a temper tantrum over Hillary Clinton not being elected and consequently any title, symbolic gesture, no matter how idiotic or in some cases violent if you talk about Antifa is justified. You're dealing with people who don't think of themselves as individuals, who think of themselves as members of an ideological high flyer, but then the school board members who I'm assuming most of whom are black, it's not even about the black community. It's about allegiance to the ideology and they're using children. That's the part of was even more damaging.

Gary: Yeah.

Nadra Enzi: That you would use children in pursuit of your blind devotion to a failed ideology because if it worked, Detroit would not be a wasteland. If it worked, New Orleans where I'm standing right now would not be a battlefield. So let's be very candid about what the life chances are for young people who have to look to persons like this for "leadership". You're mobilizing against the name on the school of a man who achieve distinction when statistically, I mean if someone were to lay odds that a bore from Detroit born to a mother who couldn't read living in the projects will become the world's number one pediatric neurosurgeon and save the lives of a pair of conjoined twins, joined up the skull and he came up with a way to separate both of them, that whole healthy and unharmed. What would, what are the odds? A billion to one? Then you're telling them black children that you shouldn't emulate somebody who beat a billion to one odds? That's racist.

Gary: No, I agree. And you know, as we get to the top of the hour, I'll, I, I'll say this, you don't have to look that far away to see how messed up society is. When you know in Baltimore, in Baltimore, the, you know, they're naming, you know, recreation centers after Freddie Gray.

Nadra Enzi: A heroin dealer.

Gary: Or a heroin dealer. I mean, you know, I think it sort of puts everything in perspective. Nadra, how can people find your, read some of your articles?

Nadra Enzi: You can find me on Twitter at N-A-D-R-A-E-N-Z-I. Or you can follow my blog and Facebook page. Urban Safetyist, that's urban safety I-S-T, one word and folks, I leave you with this thought either govern yourself or somebody else will.

Gary: Nadra, thank you for joining me this morning. It's always a pleasure and I look forward to speaking with you again.

Nadra Enzi: Likewise.

15

BRUCE HARTMAN

Gary: We have our guest on the line, Dr. Bruce Hartman. Dr. Hartman is the author of Jesus & Co.: Connecting the Lessons of The Gospel with Today's Business World. Dr. Hartman, good morning and welcome to the show.

Bruce: Good Morning Gary. Thank you for having me.

Gary: It's my pleasure. So, I was thinking Thanksgiving this year of bringing politics back to the table, and I'm not sure anyone who's having Thanksgiving with me that's listening to this is going to be happy. But my feeling is it's been a year since the president's been elected. It's time to start being able to have polite, respectful conversation. The waiting period's been long enough. For some people it's been the mourning period, and I think we have to start agreeing to learn how to agree to disagree, have civil conversations and exchange ideas without it becoming personal, and attacking one another. I know when I talk to people and I bring up the topic right away they get very defensive, and they want to go at you and have an argument, but not a discussion. And I'm okay with an argument long as, doctor, we deal with facts and not fiction, and that opinions have fine, but I want it based on fact. I may start the trend this year and just say, "Okay, enough is enough. Politics around the table at Thanksgiving." I'm not sure how well that's going to go over.

Bruce: Well, you certainly have captured the mood of what I think is the state of American politics and how people feel about it. Certainly all the polls are saying this is the most polarized our country has ever been. But in some ways though, Gary, this is actually good news. There is a wonderful website that perhaps you and your followers could sign onto, it's called Better Angels. And it's interesting that you say Thanksgiving you'd like to bring this up, because they actually have a blog on their site on how to have a good thanksgiving day meal and still be able to discuss politics. So very appropriate that you're bringing this up.

Gary: Well, I will go to their website. I'll check that out. But yeah, I think it's time.

Bruce: There's a movement going on in America that I think addresses the issue that you brought up, and the movement is to depolarize politics. Certainly, you've identified what one of the things that I see as well, is that people have prerecorded narratives. We're not listening to learn anymore. We just hear somebody say something, we hit the button, a recorded button and out comes whatever it is we want to say. But, as we both know, there are always two sides to every discussion and it was interesting. I was watching the Nixon Kennedy debates on YouTube to discover what was it like in the '60s? And even though those of us who grew up in the '60s, we thought of that debate as being tense and terse and a difficult conversation. It's actually remarkably civil to what we hear today, and I think that there is a need to return to civil discussion. One of the contents of the Gospels says to love thy neighbor. And I think if we approach each of our discussions with a true respect for the person that we're talking to, and listening to what they have to say before we talk over them, or stop listening. I think that for America, that would be the best thing we could do right now.

Gary: You bring up a point that really frustrates me and that's that prerecorded narrative. And again, Doctor, I'm okay; I love having open frank discussions with people. I love hearing other people's opinion. At the end of that conversation, my objective is to still be friends, may have learned something, and doesn't mean that he or she is going to sway me. Nor would I expect to sway them. But that prerecorded narrative without any backup to it. It's almost like we have become zombies and we don't take the time to think. It's okay to listen to someone else's opinion, or one of these narratives to go and do the investigation, and look into it. And then come up with our own perspective, or point of view on it. It's the prerecorded narrative that just makes me crazy, and then how quickly a conversation can turn nasty if someone disagrees with you.

Bruce: Yeah, and there's three things about the prerecorded narrative that we should talk about. The first is, intellectually it's really lazy to just keep saying the same thing, and I think if we all dig deeper into issues, you'll find that there are two valid arguments on either side. And the second thing is, we need to learn to respect another person's life experiences, because we enter every single discussion through a different lens. Like, Gary, your life experiences have been different than mine.

Gary: Correct.

Bruce: So to try to assume that we know everything is what creates these prerecorded narratives, but people do have different points of view and they're not created because of these people are bad, it's created because of their own life. And I think for those of us listening is understanding where the person's coming from helps you understand their argument, and the validity of their argument. The third thing, so we've talked about thinking deeper when you listen. We've talked about respecting the person's life journey, how they've walked to get to the point of view. And the third thing is knowing that none of us know 100% of the answers.

Gary: Yeah. And unfortunately, and I've been accused of this, thinking that I know all the answers. And I'd never purport to know all the answers, doctor, but there are many people out there that do. I've had conversations with people that you'd think someone programmed them and they had a live feed that they have an answer to everything. And the other thing that you just said I think I can disagree with somebody's philosophy, or what they're saying. But when you take the time to hear where they came from, or how they grew up, or what went on in their family life. Then you get the read as to why they are talking the way they do, and it's very helpful. At the end, again, we may not agree, but it is very helpful and makes you understand why they're coming where they're coming from as opposed to just making a pre-assumption about them.

Bruce: Yes. I would call this second level thinking, what we're talking about here is to move away from what our core beliefs are, and understand that they were built legitimately through our own life experiences. But so wasn't the other person's. And sometimes like in a Thanksgiving day conversation. Going around the table and just asking people what have they experienced in life is a great icebreaker to find out about people, and when you know them more humanely, you're less likely to argue or get mad at them.

Gary: Right. But why has arguing become so prominent. Well, I may know the answer to this, but this discussion has become so vicious that it's not even politics anymore, doctor. The tone is sometimes no matter what you bring up there's no civility in it anymore. It's inhumane at times that and I think it's unhealthy as a society.

Bruce: Oh it's remarkably unhealthy, and I think the word you brought up, which is the keyword, which is civility. And I think we have a responsibility to the person that we are talking to, and the person that we are listening to. To respect who they are, regardless of how we feel about them. We should think more about who they are and what they are as human beings. Part of what's created this discourse, or what I call rancor, is our politicians, in particular, they're no longer patriots. There are some, certainly in the House of Representatives and Senators. We could all admire and consider to be patriots, but we have people positioning themselves to get votes, and how they get votes is by getting money.

So there are these forces behind both the Democrats and Republicans that donate a lot of money and they expect to hear something, number one. Number two, a lot of our politicians now see their job as a career and staying employed means getting votes, and they believe creating dissent is the way to get votes. And they're listening to the extreme fringe of our country. Not the 80 to 90% that are in the middle. That's one of the reasons why there's this whole depolarization. Besides Better Angels, there's about four or five other organizations that's been set up to unify our country. But a great place to start is Better Angels, because it does get at this very issue of civility.

Gary: Yeah, I think the politics in this country have slipped to a point where it's become dangerous for the country as a whole. Sometimes when you talk about people and we have to be civil with one another, and try and be respectful of one another. It's just amazing, doctor, how many people laugh, excuse me, when I bring that up to them. That's never going to happen. That's the problem, right? When I hear that's never going to happen. That's even more alarming to me because I was like, "Are you that far gone where you can't stop and listen to what I'm saying?" We're not even having a discussion on a particular issue. We're having a discussion how we have to learn to have a discussion, which they don't even want to have at times.

Bruce: Yes. It's ironic too because none of us were raised by our parents to be a filled with rancor or an anger, and when I was a young kid my dad told me, "Gasoline never put out a fire." And I think understanding that, if you have a point of view that you want to make and that you think is important. I would start with that first, is that pouring gasoline on a fire is not going to put it out. It's only going to make it worse. So this second level thinking I think has to take that into account. That you can call somebody racist, but don't expect them to listen to you. Don't expect them to agree with you and do not expect, even if you're right, don't expect any form of conciliation on their part. I think we've lost the understanding of what name-calling and mudslinging does. So to say you can't have a discussion means that you believe that it's right to put gasoline on a fire, and I think if you think about it that way, whatever it is you're trying to do, you won't be able to get done.

Gary: No, I agree. I know, my daughter and I have some discussions at times, and I always go back to this point where they're look at it, "I have this moral and ethical compass that I live by and I listen and I change, and I'll make changes as accordingly." But certain things when we're talking about, I said, "This is where my perspective comes from." So I lead that out and I'm still open to conversation, but it doesn't mean I'm going to change, or go to someone else's point of view just for the sake of it. And I'm okay with some of that. I've had other people say to me, "Gary, because of this morally, ethically my compass is this." I'm okay with that. When you know that, that helps during the conversation.

Doctor, we're going to take a quick break and then we can return.

We're speaking with Dr. Bruce Hartman. Dr. Hartman is the author of Jesus & Co.: Connecting the Lessons of The Gospel with Today's Business World. You know, Doctor, when I was speaking about moral compass, so my point is I don't let a particular political side change me in any way. I try to stick with my belief system and people will tell me what they think I am, which always drives me absolutely crazy. "Well, you're very conservative so you believe this." No, no and I think the press has led us to go to that point, you know? The press. So the media sometimes has led us to believe that we're all being manipulated and whatever else, but my moral compass is not affected by if I disagree with someone I disagree with them and I have a certain set of standards. And I think a lot of people have lost their own standards so they don't know what those standards are.

Bruce: Yeah, that's a good point that you're bringing up about press and the media, and so this is a difficult subject. Because one, we need the press and we need the media, and it's part of what makes our democracy great. And it's one of the things that's sustained us since the signing of the constitution. So we have to be careful that we don't defer or overly criticized the media, but on the other hand, the point that you're making is very good. If I watch CNN, I know what side that I'm going to get. And if I watch Fox News, I know what side I'm going to get. And I think if the media returned back to the days of Walter Cronkite, and Chet Huntley, and David Brinkley. I think that that would subdue some of this polarization, and certainly think you're right about that. Because I do a lot of radio interviews and I think most of the folks that I talked to, I'd say at least 95%, are in the middle. But unfortunately I don't think that that's always what America sees. So I think from a political standpoint, from a media standpoint, that the standard that used to exist in journalism, I think has to come back.

Gary: Right. Oh, I agree. I agree and that I like. I want to hear both sides. I try to get guests on that lay right down the middle, and different perspectives. You should see some of the emails that I get because a lot of people assume that this is purely a one-sided radio show and they're offended when I bring someone, as they say, from the other side on. So with that said, doctor, how do we start. We touched on this, but this is a difficult process to change because it's we're getting bumped all day long with, as you say, different channel, different perspective. It's a hard job to get people to understand that you have to get back to some central point in their life, some the medium.

Bruce: Yeah, I think the first thing is we should communicate without agenda. So that's where it starts, and also our communication style I think has to change. So if you look at, we're always given two choices in life of how to be. We can either be hostile or we can be warm. That's choice number one. We make that decision. The second thing is, we can be assertive, or we can be passive. So that's the second decision that we have to make. I think all of us want to be considered warm and assertive. If you combine these two decisions that you make, right? So I think that it's fair to say that 99% of humankind wants to be considered warm and assertive, but we can't allow situations or behavior to make us hostile assertive, because it's certainly not going to accomplish anything in your communication style.

So I think that's exercise number one, is identifying those things that create in you this need to be hostile and to be overly aggressive with the communication. Likewise, what are the things that make us warm and assertive? Well, one, being the firm, but we shouldn't always wait to be affirmed.

We should always have that as a backdrop, that we are God's people, and in that God's people were made in the image of God. So we have this natural inheritance of being warm, and being assertive. And continuing to focus on that is, that is the number one thing I think we can do when in any conversation. And the more you can hang on to being warm and assertive, the closer you're going to get to getting your point made.

Gary: Yeah, I agree. And less hostility is always a great thing. We have a caller on the line who wants to ask you a question. Lee from Waltham, good morning.

Lee: Yes, thank you for taking my call. And I just want to ask you, don't you think there is a double standard that is going on right now? I mean, we're talking about all this stuff about how we have to be nice to one another and all that. We've got George Soros who's an American citizen who's a billionaire, and we know because I always hear them, how they're funneling money to these people trying to get into the country. He was responsible for the fires in the Northern Part. Oregon and Washington then after the election, and yet nothing ever happened to him. He's never brought in for sedition. He's never brought in for treason. And the same thing with Hillary Clinton. And the same thing with Barack Obama.

The thing is, I'm getting to believe there's a strata of people who cannot be touched, IE, money people versus the rest of us out here who work for a living, and we're trying to get somebody to get on our side, and they don't. I think what pushed me over the top this time, okay? Was the fact that in Florida we have so much obvious, so much corruption as far as the voting is concerned, and I think it was a test bed for what they're going to try to produce in the next election. Of how much they can get through in Broward County, and other states to get what they want. And yet no one comes to the defense. Where is the attorney general on these? Why aren't we in Florida or not we, but the supposedly the people that's supposed to back us up? And I'd like to ask these people too. Are you a conservative? And what is the conservative to these people? You ask them and they have no idea. Well, why do they call them conservative?

Gary: Let's get the doctor to respond. Thank you for the call.

Lee: Sure.

Gary: You know doctor I think the call takes on some of what we're talking about, and Lee has some points and he has his perspective. There's also at some point you've got to listen to the rhetoric and you've got to be able to decipher it. When do you think the American people, and I think part of this I hear from Lee and I hear from other callers, are listening or are listening to the media too much and not taking a break from it, because I think that's what's part of what's going on in the country today?

Bruce: Yes. I mean this is a good point that both you and the call are making. When you look at TV you can become seduced into just continuing to follow it and listen, and it's designed to do that. It's designed to keep you drawn in. So one of the things I did for one year, I didn't listen to the news or read the newspaper, and frankly, it's was not the greatest life idea and you should probably only do it for a year. But it's interesting how uncluttered you become when you don't do that. So I would only say to any caller, or any person that it is an interesting thing to try and do for short period of time. We still have to be aware of what's going on. But there was a very interesting point that the caller, Lee, made at the very beginning.

And this is one of the things that is causing the rancor. Is if you went back to the '70s and 'the 80s and you talked about political action committees, or PACs. There were very tight limits on how much a corporation, or an individual could contribute to a politician. Today, a gentleman like George Soros has a bigger voice and affects votes far more than either you or I, and it's because they pour a lot of money into the Democrats. Which is what George does. So should he really have that much power should. Should Americans allow one individual to give that much money with this very specific voice? I didn't elect George Soros to be the voice of America.

Gary: Exactly.

Bruce: Conversely the NRA is another good example, to go to the other side. The NRA, when I was a kid and I grew up in Maine, so hunting was a big deal. The NRA promoted gun safety and gun control, but now it's been taken over politically and they feed millions of dollars into our politicians as well. So the voice of the people that Washington, and Jefferson, and Adams set up has been denuded by these outside influences, because we lack the rules on how much money you can give to a politician. In turn the politician has to speak that voice of George Soros, or he doesn't get money in the next election.

Gary: Yeah, and that's exactly what it is. And no matter how, not to be negative about it, but no matter what law we may try to pass to change that, the politicians know who's feeding them and where their money's coming from. And they quickly figure out another way to fill their war chest with funds, but the point you make about taking the break from the news. I listen to a lot of the news, especially for this show, but my greatest days are when I don't listen to the news, and I just veg out from it because they wind you up. That's part of their job. They wind you up. You either agree with them and you don't agree with them and it just sets people off, but if there is something very tranquil and very nice about shutting that off for a period of time. You're doing it for a year; I give you a lot of Kudos. I'm not sure I could do it for a year, but I understand what you're saying. And I think we really need to do that. Doctor, we're at the bottom of the hour. How can people get a hold of you because I know they're going to want to look up your website or whatever?

Bruce: Well yeah, it's brucelhartman.com. It's a website that promotes my book and I would hope all the readers would be interested in doing that, and the second thing is we write blogs. We write blogs about a lot of the issues that you and I have just talked about today.

Gary: Well, I appreciate you joining me this morning. I look forward to purchasing your book and read it in full-depth, and I look forward to speaking with you again shortly.

Bruce: Yeah, I look forward to it. Thank you having me on your show.

Gary: Thank you.

16

MICHELLE OWENS

Gary: On the line with us now is Michelle Owens. Michelle is an attorney and spokesperson for SAVE- Stop Abusive and Violent Environments. She focuses on defending male students accused of sexual misconduct under Title IX. Good morning Michelle, welcome back to the show.

Michelle: Good morning. Thanks for having me back.

Gary: So you know, we have talked in the past about Title IX and the more I researched some of the things that go on it makes the hair stand up in the back of your head. But after what is going on this last week in regard to the Supreme Court, Kavanaugh, there's no doubt in my mind, Michelle, that due process is under attack right now.

Michelle: Well, it is. I mean, that's what you were saying illustrated in the media right now with Kavanaugh and Dr. Ford, there's no due process whatsoever. I tell people, I hate to see what's happening to Judge Kavanaugh, but it's a perfect illustration of what the cities I work with go through every day. I mean, it's exactly like this. You are guilty until you can prove yourself innocent and we might not even listen to all your witnesses. So good luck.

Gary: Yeah. You know, I want to get into that because when I read some of the stories that you get online and you look into some of these Title IX cases. First of all is this, what concerns me is somehow there's a culture which in law enforcement involved in the student cases that what the student has to say doesn't matter. It sort of jumped- not that they don't listen to it but they sort of jump over and they're right into conviction before investigation to put it in simple terms, which is alarming because again, there's no due process there, but what it does to families, whether it's financially, emotionally, psychologically suicide amongst individuals, it's horrific what's going on. And then for the person that made these allegations to come out and say, yeah no, it didn't happen. In cases like Massachusetts, if you're charged with one of these crimes, you know, you're on the list forever, you can't get off of it.

Michelle: Right, yeah. Well, you know, one thing that I wanted to- not really correct you but point out- is that a lot of times, most of the times when I'm dealing with these students, they do not go to law enforcement. They don't go to the police. So when they do go to the police, they actually get a more fair shot because there is more due process. Now, you are incorrect because that whole believe the victim mentality is shifting to law enforcement and you know, believe the victim sounds great. And there are certain people who should believe the victim like the counselor, your clergy, when a victim comes to you, they should believe them. But not law enforcement and not the investigating bodies of any of these organizations. Because if you believe the victim, then you automatically are saying that the accuser is guilt- the accused is guilty, which is due process gone out the window.

Gary: Right. I should retract and say a lot of that when I was reading in regard to law enforcement; it was probably campus type police situation where they got it as opposed to the local police department.

Michelle: Right. And I think they make you think when you read some of the articles that it's law enforcement. But it's not, it's a dorm advisor that saying you're guilty and investigating you. It's nothing to do with the real criminal justice system. And that's what is so alarming is that we are telling these boys that they are guilty of a felony, of rape or sexual assault, but they aren't getting due process, which you would get if you went through the court system and the general public doesn't understand that. And that's one reason, you know, not that I was happy about what happened with Kavanaugh, but it was such a great illustration for everyone that doesn't understand. And the people I've talked to have said oh, is this really what it's like for boys on campus? And I said yes, and you know not just boys on campus, because I've represented any administrators on campus, any people who work, employees, professors, and then it's spreading out to the general population in the workforce as well. So it's a horrific thing.

Gary: Yeah. I mean, there's no doubt that this is not good on college campuses, but how do they get away with these quote unquote kangaroo type courts on these college campuses?

Michelle: Well, it's because there's no rules right now. That's one thing that we are anticipating, is the new regulations that Betsy DeVos is going to present, hopefully saying regarding Title IX because until now, what she's going to do, there has never been a system in place that regulates it fairly or regulates it consistently throughout the universities and colleges. And that's what I think will help, because I think she's making some major changes from what the Obama administration had put into force that wasn't really law because it really didn't go through the proper channels. But needless to say, it was being enforced anyway on the colleges.

Gary: Right.

Michelle: Because they're afraid of losing their federal funding. I mean, that's what it all boils down to, is money.

Gary: Right. So they're afraid of the federal funding which leads me to ask you, is there a push on college campuses, for administrators or staff to encourage this type of, you know, reporting? Believe me, if having a daughter, sisters, whatever, no one wants their child to ever be sexually assaulted, nothing to happen and you want them to report it. But reading some of the articles that I did, Michelle, it's almost like there's an over push, an overreaction at times.

Michelle: Well there is, I mean they have- what I call it is propaganda. I mean it's almost like it's cult-like behavior where these women are going to seminars put on by the campus, the Title IX department, and they're being told that they had been sexually assaulted, that when you felt bad after you left that sexual encounter, that was sexual assault. Where these girls beforehand had no idea that, you know, they just thought it was a bad date or you know, the guy was a jerk, whatever, which is what the truth is. But they leave thinking oh wait, he was a jerk to me and now I can do something to him, you know, get back to him in some way. And yes, there is a huge push and it's being funded by a group called Violence Against Women International. I'm sure it does some good things and I've only focused on that that they've done, but they are behind the believe the victim campaign and they are the ones who give the money to support it and to put out the pamphlets and information to help the schools teach it, and that's what they do.

Gary: Yeah. And the schools run with that propaganda, basically.

Michelle: Because they have a very liberal feminist in charge of a Title IX department who has personal beliefs that are in line with that. So they do it, not really at the nudging of the university, but because they've been hired by the university and it's what they want to do.

Gary: A lot of times these result in wrongful convictions, well never mind- false allegations, but sometimes wrongful convictions and from there it's completely downhill for those involved.

Michelle: Well, if you get kicked out of school then as after a Title IX, if you're found responsible is what they call it for a Title IX claim or charge, then you cannot get into another school absent lying on your application, or trying really really hard and you know, going to a really lower tier school. So it's very difficult to finish your education at all. And that's the problem is that the boys can't get a four-year degree, much less graduate school. So you're kind of stopping them in their tracks educationally. And that is a really big deal when you think about it because you have boys, some of them, you know I represented people who had full rides to MIT that you know, for graduate school, that was on the line and that's going to change your whole trajectory for life. If you can't get into the program you were intending to go through and be what you thought you were going to be. Doctors, the same thing, I've represented students who are going into their fellowship or going- applying for their residencies and if you get stopped right there, what do you do? You know, what do you do with a medical school degree that you can't use?

Gary: Yeah, I know, it's totally horrific. You know, it's obviously the Title IX creates this reduced due process to individuals.

Michelle: Yeah. It's pretty much absent due process at this point. There are very few schools, and I've worked across the country, I represent students across the country because I can't act as an attorney, I can only act as an advisor. You're not allowed to have an attorney speak for you, so there's no cross examination, no due process. I've seen a lot of schools and how they handle it and none of them, with the exception of maybe two that I've dealt with, have been fair at all. That's what people- I don't think people know what due process really is. I don't think I really did before I went to law school, but it's just being fair.

Gary: Right.

Michelle: It's making sure that the system is fair to both sides and it's pretty much common sense, but that is what's lacking completely.

Gary: So the school is the judge, the jury and they hand out whatever the conviction is, that's it.

Michelle: Yeah. Judge, jury, investigator, judge, and jury.

Gary: Yup. And that's probably where I was going originally with the investigation part of it. And you're not allowed to represent, you can only advise. You can't represent the client in there? They're not allowed to have legal representation?

Michelle: Right, right. But it is important that a student have an attorney, I don't want to downplay that because what I do is what the school is supposed to do. I do the investigation and I talk to the witnesses and I make sure that the student that I'm representing has all of the witnesses that they can get because, you know, I did this for a living so I know what to look for and I know what matters as a witness and sees, you know, 19-year-old boys that are under stress don't know. So oftentimes I'm successful at the administrative area because I come in there with something they're not expecting and that is some actual evidence that is hard to overlook, and that they look at it and say okay, we really don't think he did this and we know that we're going to have a lawsuit if we don't decide it right. I have a pretty high success rate if I can get involved at the beginning.

Gary: Yeah, I know, I assume that's the most important time. We're going to take a quick break and when we return we'll continue the conversation.

Gary: We're speaking with attorney Michelle Owens. Michelle is an expert in university Title IX cases. Michelle, where did this victim culture come from? How did it come to the point it is today?

Michelle: That's a really good question, and I think it comes from social media because somehow, the me-too movement, I think is where it began- which is funded by the way, in part by the group I told you about earlier- but that made it where it's a badge of honor to be a victim. And right now it is the best thing that you can do is be a victim. You're in the in crowd; you're popular if you're a victim. And it's interesting because, you know, I'm a therapist before I went to law school, that was my first career, and we would, you know, had training and we would teach people that you don't have to be a victim, that being a victim is not good. There's an option because it takes control away from your life, it takes away your responsibility and your ability to do things when you're the victim.

Michelle: But now we have these people who are the victim and they want to be. And what it does, I think it caught on because it takes away responsibility from the woman. If a girl has made a bad choice in a sexual encounter or you know, in the workplace. And I'm not discounting, I want to make a disclaimer that I know there are real sexual assaults of rape, and I would never discount that. I have friends who've been raped and it's horrific. But what we're seeing are a lot, and I mean a lot of false accusations. What it does is it takes away all responsibility from the woman and that's very appealing. If you've done something that you don't feel good about, and all of a sudden you can blame it on the guy and you're the victim, then there's no responsibility. So I think that's where it comes from. It's appealing and it's the in thing right now.

Gary: And it ruins, you know, the bottom line here, Michelle, is that it's ruining lives, people are spending time either, like you said losing opportunities that never should have come about or maybe spending time in jail. I think we really have to stop this victim culture or get to the bottom of it, or this is going to get a lot worse as we go forward.

Michelle: Well, it's getting worse for women in general right now because what's happening is no one wants work with women. I mean, I would not advise any of my clients who are self-employed and hiring someone to hire a woman because... or if they did, they're going to have to have somebody there with them all the time, because if you fire her, the first thing she's going to say is that you sexually assaulted her. You know, that's the thing you do these days. So it's very dangerous and it's actually hurting, you know, the women's movement and the feminist movement more than they even imagined. They can't fathom how much it's hurting that movement.

Gary: Yeah. And you know, you listen to stories of people that have been wrongfully committed and you try to think about this when somehow, someone comes about and said, oh, I was not telling the truth, so they'll let out of jail. Never mind, you know, the fact that their lives are ruined, they're sitting in jail.

Michelle: Right.

Gary: For myself, it's hard to wrap my hands around it and you feel so horrific for that person. How do you make that person's life whole? You can't, Michelle.

Michelle: No you can't. And the only thing you can do is give them some money. Well that doesn't make up for the fact that, you know, the Duke Lacrosse players, most people haven't really followed the story and don't know they're innocent. I mean, you know, most people, some people, and so when you think Duke Lacrosse, you think, oh rapist. So if any one of those guys applied for a job, it's going to hurt them. Anything they do, it's going to affect them because there is a negativity that surrounded them despite the fact that they were exonerated. You just can't unring the bell, as we say in the legal world. You can't take it back once it's there. And I don't know a way to fix it. There's not a way, there's not enough money in the world that can repair relationships and your reputation.

Gary: Yeah. And as we've seen with the Kavanaugh hearings, even when the facts show that nothing, they could not corroborate any of the evidence, there are many people out there that are still saying guilty, guilty, guilty. That is very concerning to me because that to me is part ignorance. I hate to use that term, but it's part ignorance and it's a culture that is going to take a while to fix and you've got to change that culture. You've got to change that thought process. But a lot of times the media and other entities, other bodies are not helping change that. They're promoting it.

Michelle: Well, they are promoting it. I feel like, it's almost a tribe mentality between the Republicans and Democrats right now, and no one listens to reason. I'm very logical and apolitical and I love it when I see somebody from the other side of the aisle talk positively about somebody who's the opposite of what they are, Republican or Democrat because I think that's the way it should be. You should be able to logically listen to each other's opinions. But that's not happening. If you are a woman and someone has said that they are sexually assaulted and you're in this group of, you know, where you believe that, you're following this me too and believe the victim, then you're going to believe that they were sexually assaulted regardless of the evidence placed in front of me.

And those are the types of people that are deciding these cases in schools. And so you can see why it's so impossible to get any kind of a fair hearing there. When you get into court, it's very different. Just as an aside, I don't know if you have heard about, I think it was Sacred Heart. There was a woman who accused two football players of sexual assault, but she went to the police, which was good for them and bad for her because I don't remember if she admitted later, or if they found out she was lying and she admitted it, but she's spending time in jail because of it. And that is a good deterrent right there, and so their lives were not nearly as horribly affected as most people's because it was found out early and she's being punished for it, which gives some credibility to what they were saying.

Gary: Right. And I think that is needed in society on so many different levels, but you know, if you make a statement and it's not true, you have to be held accountable and legally you have to pay the price. And I think if we would see more of that, it's not gonna stop this completely, but it's going to make someone think twice that if I'm make- telling a lie and I can end up in jail, that I'd better think twice about what I'm saying.

Michelle: Yeah. And you know what? I just have to say what's happening. One of my cases recently, I just can't even imagine this, this guy was found guilty. He had someone that was his, you know, friends with benefits is what they called it and they basically were sexual partners and not boyfriend, girlfriend and they have sex. I mean like 80 times and in the middle of that time period, one time she makes the claim that it was not consensual and I don't- somebody put her up to it.

I don't know why, something happened, but they disregarded the fact that she had sex with him some 40 times after that and said that he raped her that time. I mean, who goes back for more if you were raped? She keeps going back to the guy 40 times. Those are the kind of cases that you're seeing where the guys are found responsible.

Gary: Yeah, I think it's a difficult time for young men and young men in college especially. You send your child to college, there's all the worries of a number of different things. But I think this has to be top on the list right now Michelle, one of the major concerns.

Michelle: Well it needs to be for parents of boys, it really does need to be the top concern they have because it's the scariest thing for them. And I have twins, I have a boy and a girl that will be off to college soon and I am much more concerned about my son. I've taught my daughter not to be in certain situations where you could be raped and you could be assaulted, you could lose control, but I'm not worried about her. I'm worried about my son because he could do nothing and be accused. He could not, you know, he could turn someone down for a date and be accused and they're going to believe her at the beginning.

Gary: And that's why, on the other side as far as the female students have to understand that if you make a false statement, there could be a serious problem on your hand. Especially if it ends up, like you said, if it's lucky enough to end up with law enforcement and not college law enforcement, I think there's a different side to that. But this is just; this is... a lot of this-

Michelle: It's scary.

Gary: What's that? It's very scary-

Michelle: It's scary.

Gary: Is this administration, President Trump, changing some of this stuff or is his administration trying to-

Michelle: No he is, he is definitely changing it. Regardless of anyone's political belief, if you have a son, you should be very glad that we have Betsy DeVos in the Department of Education right now, because she recognized the problem early on and listened to boys who were saying look, this is what's happening to us. It is ruining our lives and she is making changes. You'll soon, the new Title IX regulations will come out and they will be law and they will be in force and applicable to all schools that take any kind of federal funding, which as far as I found so far is every school.

Gary: I was going to say it has to be all of them, yeah.

Michelle: Yeah, because you get loans, student loans. It will be applicable and it's going to make things more fair. We don't know what they are yet, but we know the direction that they're going. So yes, this administration is changing it through the Department of Education.

Gary: Yeah. That's insane, because we are having colleges and universities become the justice system in such an unequal manner is very scary. And as a parent, my daughter is through with college and gone through that, but having a son, if I had a son going through college right now, I'd be very, very concerned. Michelle, how can people get in touch with you or read some of your stuff?

Michelle: They can find me at my, if they just Google, Michelle Owens attorney, they will find my website, and also I'm on Instagram, attorneymichelleowens.

Gary: Well Michelle, thank you for joining us in and thank you for the great work you're doing on this, because somebody has to advocate for these young men out there who, many of their lives. And as I said early, not just their lives, their families, have been dis- gone through bankruptcy trying to defend them, so. Heartbreaking.

Michelle: Save Services too, who I'm the spokesperson for, because they have a lot of great information on their website for families to educate themselves.

Gary: Thank you, Michelle. Have a wonderful day.

Michelle: Thanks.

17

MEGAN BARTH

Gary: On the line with us now is Megan Barth. Megan is the co-chair of Red Wave America Pac and the Media Equality Project. She serves as National Spokeswoman for mediaequalizer.com. Megan, good morning and welcome to the show.

Megan: Good morning. Thanks for having me.

Gary: So a number of things I wanna talk to you about, but I wanna first focus on Florida and this Ms. Snipes, this Board of Elections who's in charge of the Board of Elections down in, I believe it's Broward and what's going on down there. And we've had callers call in already this morning saying, "Oh, they're gonna steal the election from the Republicans," and, "How can this be happening again?" First of all, how is this woman still holding that position, Megan, based on her past history?

Megan: Well she's a Democrat so you can be a criminal and get away with it.

Gary: Yeah.

Megan: We have Brenda Snipes who was caught in 2016 destroying ballots who is now in charge of ballots and counting ballots, that makes complete sense doesn't it Gary? And I'm sure that your listeners are saying, "Well of course, why not?" Well, no. Anybody with an ounce of common sense and decency would say that she should not be in that position. What we are witnessing is ballot harvesting. I've written about voter fraud since 2016 when I caught a massive amount of suspicious activity in the Nevada election.

Gary: I remember that, yeah.

Megan: We had. Oh, okay. Oh, very good.

Gary: Yep.

Megan: And so I said, "You know, what I think I'm witnessing here is a template of fraud. A template that could be taken to each and every precinct, each and every state in order to flip elections by narrow margins or even by larger margins." And why is it that every time these ballots are mysteriously found or mysteriously appear, 90% of them always tend to lean Democrat? And it's only in the elections that the Democrats are losing, they never find ballots when they've won elections. It just doesn't make sense and when something doesn't make sense it's not true.

And your callers are absolutely right because the template of fraud I uncovered in Nevada is very similar to what's going on in Florida, it's very similar to what's going on in Arizona and also I think Georgia is now confirmed, but they probably would have tried it there. But what I've said since 2016 is that when you see massive amounts of voter registration, and we saw massive amounts of voter registration this midterm cycle. 50 states, all of our states, do not require or check for citizenship of registered voters, not one state. Now each of these voters, whether they're fraudulent or not, that are registered will get ballots. They'll get sample ballots, they'll get absentee ballots and what happens to those ballots especially if they're in the wrong hands and in the hands of a fraudulent voter? Well they can be used to vote and no one checks for ID, very few states do I think there's four of the books.

Gary: Yeah-

Megan: And so what we're witnessing is a massive amount of fraud and the Democrats, once again, trying to steal the election in one of the most corrupt counties in our Republic which is Broward county, the home of Debbie Wasserman Schultz.

Gary: Right, the home of Debbie Wasserman Schultz. And it's amazing, Megan, how immediately she's tried to turn this into a race issue.

Megan: Well of course because everything's race.

Gary: Everything's race. Yeah, I mean everything's race. Now she has 'til 10 o'clock this morning to comply with this court order that she claims she's not going to. So it's gonna be interesting to see how this thing unfolds, but it's one thing to have fraud, unacceptable, but to have the same woman in place who we know has been caught doing this in the past and I hate to use the word common sense 'cause it doesn't prevail anymore, but it's like how can this be happening again?

Megan: Right, and I asked that very question on my Facebook page. I have a personal page, ReaganBabe, Reagan as in Ronald, Babe as in Ruth-

Gary: Right.

Megan: and that's also my personal blog that I had started a few years ago when I was witnessing the mainstream media completely ignore the facts and use Democrat talking points as headlines. I said, "You know what, I'm gonna start writing about the truth," and it worked out. But nonetheless, we have Florida that will or could easily be stolen and if this does not call for massive changes in our entire voter registration and our entire voting system, the Democrats will continue to steal. They believe that if they steal Florida they will steal the 2020 election. Florida is extraordinarily important, as well as Texas, as well as Arizona, every election is important and obviously it's very important when the Democrats have to break the law in order to win elections. I was watching Twitter feeds, et cetera last night as I was flying back from D.C. and the dumpster fire NPR that we pay for with our tax dollars had a headline that said, "Even though Donald Trump said that there's widespread voter fraud, no evidence exists for him to make those claims."

Gary: Yeah, that's-

Megan: Well maybe because there has been no widespread investigation.

Gary: Right, right. Yeah, I saw that and my eyes almost plunges out of my head when I read that. It's absolutely ludicrous, absolutely so-

Megan: And that's the same headline you'll find at CNN coming out of Jake Tapper's mouth or Don Lemon's mouth if anyone's still watching CNN. The only people that really watch CNN are the ones that are forced to while sitting in an airport. I was in three airports, four airports actually, over this past week and every single airport had CNN on and I kept saying, "Geez, I wonder what they're ratings would be? Would they be worse than what they are now if we weren't forced to watch them in the airport?" But nonetheless, voter fraud is real, election fraud is real and we know that because what we are seeing with our own eyes as the criminal who should have been criminally charged in 2016 in charge of ballots and counting ballots in 2018.

Gary: Yeah, yeah. It's horrific, it's horrific. On another note, Jeff Sessions, are you glad he's gone?

Megan: I think everyone's glad he's gone expect the coordinated mobs that Rachel Maddow is trying to coordinate in New York. I think everyone's glad he's gone. We had a lot more expectations of Jeff Sessions, we certainly didn't expect him to recuse himself and it's interesting that Democrats never recuse themselves, Robert Mueller should have recused himself, Rosenstein should have recused himself, James Comey should have recused himself, the list goes on, and on and on. So plenty of Democrats have been compromised from a legal standpoint and ethical standpoint, but when you aren't operating in a world of ethics, specifically politics, the Democrats won't recuse themselves, but now are calling for the new acting AG to recuse himself.

Gary: Right, it's hypocrisy.

Megan: So-

Gary: Yeah, hypocrisy. And you know what I find even more interesting? Sessions, I don't know if you saw this after Wednesday when he was being interviewed, acknowledged that the length of the Mueller investigation is unhealthy. Really? I'm like, "You're saying this now? You're out of office and now you're saying this? That's what everybody's been telling you for the last two years.

Megan: Right, two years and we still have, what happened to the old Russia collusion narrative, where did that go? I haven't heard Russia collusion. Is Brenda Snipes Russian because she's certainly interfering in the election in Florida? We haven't heard one word about the core issue and the allegations and the charges that sucked the oxygen out of every room for close to two years.

Gary:

Right, right. Though I did get into a very heated debate with somebody the other day over Russia collusion when we were talking about the President and him having the exchange with the CNN reporter and this gentleman's telling me, "Well, do you know why he did that?" I'm like, "Well, you tell me why?" He said, "Because he wants to hide the Russian collusion issue." And I'm like, "Seriously, after two years?" I don't care how hard left you are, you cannot believe that there's anything going on with Russia or it would have been out there and it would have been over by now. It's sad to think that some people still believe that, Megan.

Megan:

Yeah, the whole narrative was manufactured by the Democrat party, specifically Adam Schiff and others. Now Adam Schiff is gonna chair the intelligence committee, geez, what could go wrong? And they manufactured this narrative, they continued to repeat the lie until the lie was then believed to be the truth. It's good old Alinsky tactic, good old Saul Alinsky tactic, to just keep pushing the lie and pushing the lie until it breaks through to the truth. It's astounding how fast people are without any evidence and just allegation they are ready to destroy anyone's life like Brett Kavanaugh for example, we now know that at least a couple women have admitted that they are absolute lying frauds. But the Democrats will destroy the Fourth Amendment just as quick as they'll destroy the First Amendment, and the Second Amendment, and the Sixth Amendment in order to achieve unilateral power. And so we should not be surprised that a political party who believes that the Constitution is a living and breathing document according to their whims it needs to be changed, would go after their political enemies through their abuse of that very document.

Gary:

Megan, we've gotta take a quick break, but when we return I do wanna ask you a few more questions about the press and talk about this divide in the country if we can ever come together.

On the line with us is Megan Barth. Megan is the co-chair of Red Wave America Pac and the Media Quality Project, she serves as a national spokeswoman for mediaequalizer.com. Megan, that news conference, I think, said it all the other day and I love the way the President handled it. But this can't go on 'cause this media fiasco is just ridiculous and I'm not sure how they have to handle it, but I think they started by pulling the press pass initially of Acosta there and trying to move forward. But it's a media circus and those that wanna ask intelligent questions are shunned and outnumbered by these lunatics.

Megan: Yeah, there's an old saying in the debate that it's not the question that's asked, it's how-

Gary: Right.

Megan: The question is asked. And so when you have headlines or questions dripping with bias, loaded questions that insert signals of bias and words of bias, then the answer is already predetermined or at least they want to predetermine the President's answer and then they try to narrowly ask the question with bias or to put him in a corner and try to disprove a negative, right?

Gary: Right.

Megan: So that is the problem. We never witnessed this we're not even witnessing any scrutiny of the high crimes in the community of Democrats. The Democrats are protected and when you don't have an objective press that's what happens, propaganda are of the Democrat party which is the mainstream media. They use the mainstream media in order to protect themselves. And we can't forget Jonathan Gruber who I think it's out of your neck of the woods.

Gary: Right.

Megan: And he was the one that was the architect of Obamacare, one of them. And on a mic he basically had said that the Democrats relied on the stupidity of the American people in order to pass Obamacare. Well who assists in the stupidity of the American people? Well it's the mainstream media because if they aren't reporting the truth, if they're reporting nothing but propaganda, then you have a lot of people who lack the knowledge to make educated decisions. For example, your friend who believes in this whole Russia collusion scenario even though there's no proof to back it up. Actually the only proof that was ever found was Russia spent 10 grand on some Facebook ads against Hillary Clinton and against Donald Trump. And so when you look at the coverage that the mainstream media provides, it's not the coverage of the facts, it's not the coverage of the truth, it's to give coverage to the Democrat party and provide coverage.

Gary: Yeah, they developed a narrative and then they provide the coverage to prove the narrative to persuade people is what they're doing.

Megan: Right.

Gary: Yeah.

Megan: Exactly.

Gary: Yeah, it's crazy. One of the things, the incident at Tucker Carlson's house the other night. Put your politics aside, that behavior cannot go on. And when I have conversations with people and they're defending this and they tell me not to use the word mob, first of all I used it and much more because I will not concede to political correctness 'cause I think that's what they're trying to do, make that word "bad" so you can't say it anymore. But this is just unacceptable and it has to be dealt with 'cause this, to me, is going to worse before it gets better, Megan.

Megan: Yeah, it will get worse. An inherent action of socialism is balance and force, right?

Gary: Right.

Megan: So you cannot institute socialism without violence and you cannot institute socialism without force. And so what we're witnessing is a very well-funded Democrat mob. I love the word mob, I also love the word Soros, but when I would mention the word all the sudden the left is accusing me of being an anti-Semite. There's a lot of dog whistles and the left believes that they own the language. Do they have their own dictionary that I'm supposed to read and abide by? Well, no, I'm not going to abide when I wanna call it like I see it. And that's exactly why President Trump was elected because he called things like he saw things. He was finally saying things that many Americans wanted to say, but were afraid to say.

Gary: Right.

Megan: Many things related to immigration, many things related to the economy, many things related to the wars, many things related to trade, et cetera. And so these violent mobs are simply paramilitary arms of the Democrat party and they're very well funded. And so what needs to happen that's from a law and order standpoint is we need to make sure that we rip the mask off these white, spoiled children and they're not allowed to wear masks when they're creating terror and creating havoc on the street across the country and in front of people's homes and threatening innocent people, that's number one. Number two, you rip off the mask and then what you do is you rip off the funding. You freeze all the assets of George Soros and his 184 different 501c3's that illegally operate in this country that fund the overthrow of capitalism because that's what this is about. Whether it's the migrant mob that's going to invade our southern border or wants to invade our southern border, or if it's the violent mobs that we witness on the streets whether it's in Berkeley or in front of Tucker Carlson's house, they're well-funded and so we need to freeze the assets by which these groups are operating and are being protected by.

Gary: Yes. Yeah, I couldn't agree more and another thing you said, forget about what dictionary they use, you have to use the words that appropriately describe the action and you can't be afraid of that. I had someone say to me the other morning that, "I can't believe you say the things that you say." I'm like, "What, the truth?"

Megan: Right.

Gary: And it's amazing that people are so afraid nowadays, "If I said that at work my job would be in jeopardy." Well you've got a problem then. If you can't tell the truth, Megan, then we might as well stop right there. It's crazy, it's insane.

Megan: Yeah, I often will. When I'm on radio and if I'm hosting radio I will use, of course, the term illegal alien, and I was using that term with an elected Democrat, I believe his name was Michael Blake and he's part of the DNC, and he was chastising me like, "Don't use the word illegal alien." And I said, "Well look, pal," I go, "Your party was in power for eight years, you had unilateral power for multiple years within that eight years, you could have changed the law. I'm reading the law, the law says illegal alien and that's exactly the term I'm going to use."

Gary: Yeah.

Megan: Whether it's illegal alien, or whether it's mob, or whether it's George Soros, they want to silence you. There is no such thing as hate speech, there is no such thing as hate speech. Hate speech was a manufactured term by the Democrats in order to scare people who disagree with them. Hate speech is a subjective meaning. They're offended by the word mob.

Gary: Right. It could be any other word; it could be-

Megan: It could be any word.

Gary: Tomorrow it's gonna be another word, Megan, that's-

Megan: Correct.

Gary: 'Cause they're ideal is shut us down, to keep us quiet and they do it through fear and whether it's through general fear or fear at the workplace, fear econo- whatever the case is, but you just can't concede to that type of behavior. I know I refuse to and I never will but it has to be confronted 'cause when I talk to people and they're allowing this to go on I'm like, "Well what do you really believe?" "Well I'm just afraid." Well you can't be afraid 'cause if you're afraid you're gonna end up giving your rights up, more and more of your rights up sooner or later.

Megan: Yeah, the Democrats want you to be fearful so you shut up, but the Democrats operate in a vacuum of fear, if you will, they need fear, fear creates dependency. So when they create chaos, they create fear and then they say fear is dependency and so we've heard this time and time again is that dependency is extraordinarily important to the Democrats, why? Because dependency creates a generation of dependency and it also fuels the bigger bureaucracy and the bigger the government, the happier the Democrats.

Gary: Right, the happier the Democrat, the more money they can take from us and-

Megan: Correct.

Gary: ... yeah, it's a viscous circle. Megan, how can people find you and get a hold of you?

Megan: Mediaequalizer.com, ReaganBabe.com, Reagan as in Ronald, Babe as in Ruth, ReaganBabe.com and Red Wave America Pac. All of those can be found on Facebook as well as our coordinating websites.

Gary: Well I appreciate you joining me this morning and I look forward to speaking to you again as things progress.

Megan: Very good.

Gary: Thank you, Megan.

Megan: Thank you so much.

18

RENEE JOLLY

Gary: Renee Jolly, Renee is the parent of a son who was falsely accused by a female student and wrongfully expelled from his university. Renee believes in fairness and due process for all students on university campuses across the nation.

Renee, good morning and welcome to the show.

Renee: Good morning, Gary. Thanks for having me on.

Gary: It's my pleasure and I'll just quickly fill you in. I've done quite a few shows on Title IX and had some great experts on and opened my eyes to things that I was totally unaware of.

Last week there was another show on the station that they had a guest in the studio that talked about Title IX and our show got pulled in because we've had experts on. I received numerous emails last weekend from people wanting to talk about it. Nobody in their right mind supports anyone who would commit that type of crime. One of the things that has always bothered me is the accused, the way that Title IX system has been set up, the accused is done before it even gets started.

When I started investigating, looking at what it did to ones' lives, whether it's the student, the student's family, his friends, not being able to get back into school, their reputation in some states like Massachusetts that CORI never is removed and their lives are ruined. I said, "There's something wrong here and it has to change."

Massachusetts, I don't know if they passed a new law or they're trying to pass through the law to try and protect within the guidelines of the new federal law, which always makes me scary when the state does that.

But I wanted to talk to you first of all about your son's experience and what you and your family went through, and then some of the new Title IX permissions.

Renee: Sure, absolutely. I appreciate being on because really my intention is twofold. I want to help the listener understand what's really going on college campuses and then, once they understand, to be vocal and educate not only their own students but anybody they know going to college, what's happening.

Renee: Also, like you said, secondly talk about the importance of thoughtful reasons civil debate on this campus sexual assault issue because just because a student like my son stepped onto a college campus, it shouldn't mean that they lose their constitutional rights. Yet that's exactly what's happening and the fight began initially for my son but for me it's evolved into all wrongfully, falsely accused students. There's hundreds and thousands of them.

Gary: Let's talk about your son and when this happened and what happened.

Renee: My son's case is still under investigation at his university by the Department of Education Office of Civil Rights so I don't want to say too much but I want to tell enough so that the listener understands what's going on.

Gary: Perfect, I get it.

Renee: I'll start with the unexpected email that my son received from the university Student Conduct Office.

It was emailed to him to come into the Student Conduct Office to meet and discuss a potential violation of sexual misconduct. He had no idea what it was for.

The email didn't tell him any specific information like what he was being accused of, who was accusing him, what incident was in question, or even when this incident occurred.

He had the opportunity to bring along a support person so he brought along a friend. This meeting was about 30 minutes long and it was his only opportunity to ever have a one-on-one conversation before he was expelled from the university.

Renee: He had no opportunity to prepare. He never got a hearing or a question or cross-examination opportunity. What my son learned from that meeting was it was a night in question with a sexual interaction about two months before. Both the accuser and my son were drinking but interestingly, for his case, there were two eyewitnesses, two of his friends that walked in the room during the encounter and what they saw was my son was the one passed out on his back with her on top.

The next morning my son woke up with hickeys all over his neck that he didn't even remember receiving and there's photographic evidence of that.

His accuser made a claim when very likely the reverse could potentially be true. Even though there were direct eyewitness statements and photographs, and even her own friends who were involved in the situation, not the actual interaction but involved in that evening, stated differently, supporting my son's side of the story. But the school ignored the evidence, including photographic.

The interesting thing when his friends walked in on the interaction, my son gave their names after he learned what the incident was. He gave their names so that they were called in to give their testimony. It really wasn't testimony; it was a conversation.

The 16-page investigative report that was given from the school stated that they didn't believe their claims because they shared nearly identical versions of what they saw and the Title IX administrator wrote in the final report that since their stories were so similar and they were his friends, they must be lying.

Gary: Unbelievable.

Renee: Yet, had their stories contradicted one another, they would have also been seen as not credible. So there was absolutely no way for my son to prove his innocence because they had already decided his fate long before it was over.

When we read the final investigative report, exculpatory evidence was left off that corroborated his side of the story. The photograph with the hickeys that were ultimately shared with the Title IX office, they were discounted because they said that was just a moment in time, it doesn't prove anything.

My son and other students have expressed during this process that they feel they're being set up by their institution that's their only hope for justice because no matter what he said or did, there was no way that he could clear himself. No matter what text messages show, no matter how openly and honestly they tell the truth, the likelihood in today's university campus culture is you're found responsible even if the evidence is on your side.

You don't realize that until you know somebody or your own child has gone through this process and you see the unfairness.

Gary: Having spoken to people, thank god my daughter's done with college and in her profession, but talking to people who have children in college or grandchildren or whatever the case may be, and you tell them about this and Renee, they look at you like you're telling them a lie. Like "No, that type of non-due process doesn't happen in this country."

Unfortunately, a lot of them get a rude awakening at some point. If it's a parent or a grandparent asking, someone asking for money to help defend or whatever the case may be, what's really going on.

I don't want to get into specifics because your case is still; you're moving it along but my concern is these Title IX administrators. I think there's a conflict of interest there because the university is paying them and they know what they have to do for the university to continue to get its federal funding. But their training and what their background is and what makes them experts, it just can't be a number of classes they sit in.

But that's basically what it is. It's minimal training. In my son's situation it was a single investigator model. It was basically one person who was the judge and the jury and the decision, like you said, was made long before. The outcome of this case was decided before it fully even started.

My son's university was one of the first 50 universities who were under an Office of Civil Rights investigation stemming from that 2011 Dear Colleague letter that I know you've discussed in the past and his particular school ran the risk of losing about $42 million in federal funding annually.

Renee: So there's such intense pressure on them that they didn't care if they were expelling an innocent student as much as they cared about their reputation and their federal funding.

Gary: Right, we discussed this. We had a guest on prior to you who were expelled, thrown out of West Point after being falsely accused.

You look at the colleges, Renee, and they're doing this cost-benefit analysis: keep the federal funding and deal with a lawsuit if someone can afford a lawsuit.

: The consensus is it's less money for us to keep going with Title IX and pay out those that we have to if we lose a lawsuit here or there. That's just so wrong on so many different levels, Renee.

Renee: Yes, I listened to the speaker before, Trent. And very similar to his story, my son was the same thing. When he was emailed to come in, he didn't even call us at that point because he thought, "Well, I didn't do anything wrong. So if I just tell the truth, it'll be okay."

When he had that initial meeting, which was in the fall, it was a little over two months later before he got the email saying, "You've been found guilty of basically sexual assault by force." Which the politically correct word is sexual assault but really that is rape by definition.

When he called us, he's across the country from where we were, it's a private university that he was on full ride scholarship for. The last thing you expect is a phone call late on a Friday night from your son who's across the country saying he's being accused of sexually assaulting another student and then ultimately have the entire trajectory of his future changed so we got involved at that point.

Again, we're across the country so it was a Friday. On Monday morning we're on the phone trying to get a copy of the investigative report, he hadn't even seen it from the school. Finding out who do we hire for an attorney. At this point, like you had mentioned before, we really as parents were not educated on Title IX. He was a sophomore but during freshman orientation, we actually didn't even go to the student conduct portion because we thought he doesn't really have a problem, he's never had a problem with student conduct.

Renee: So we weren't educated on Title IX. So we called a criminal attorney who worked with civil rights attorney and a private investigator to, during the appeal process, which is about a three-week process for schools to appeal their decision. The private investigator went on campus, interviewed more students, got more evidence. But again, the outcome of this case was decided already. There was nothing we've learned.

This was several years ago so it was early on in the process and a lot more has been known now. I've educated myself so that's really what I hope to do with the listeners is give them more education now than I had in the past so they can jump on it quickly.

Gary: You talk about student conduct. I read something very interesting the other day it goes on at school.

Your parents bring you there to drop you off or orientation, whatever the case may be, and they sit in the student conduct meeting, totally different from the ones that some schools, I'm not painting with a broad brush, give to the students that almost outline how they should file these sexual assault claims.

The presumption is right there, they're laying it out, they're putting it in their minds before it even happens or, if it does even happen. If these things happen, you have the right to do this, this, and this.

It's okay to explain to them the process, but I think they're going beyond that, Renee, and pushing the table a little bit. That's what concerns me about these Title IX administrators.

Renee: Right, yes, the mentality in the training that the administrators get on campus is start by believing.

Renee: In a criminal justice system, even a university tribunal system, when you believe the accuser outright, by default in effect you're disbelieving the respondent.

In a justice system, you can't start by believing but I say, "Let's start by receiving." Receive the accusation open-mindedly without judgment, without predetermination, then do a thorough investigation, gather all the evidence, and then and only then will you know who to believe.

Believe the accuser I think has a place in the counseling department but not in the court of law and certainly not on a campus tribunal.

Gary: Excuse me for one second but the accuser, the questions that are when they're interviewing he or she, they're very leading and they're not dismissing the facts. They're right away, like you say, assuming it happened, so they've taken away that line of questioning that someone trained in law enforcement may be able to first respond with.

Right, and I know and I want to fully respect and show empathy because there are true victims of sexual assault and those perpetrators need to be put behind bars and taken care of. But just because somebody says something happened doesn't mean it's true and that's why it's so important to have due process and cross-examination.

I heard you ask Trent "How are we going to combat these false allegations?" I don't know that we ever will be able to fully stop false allegations. Women lie, men lie, everybody lies. Always have and always will since the beginning of time but I think we can start by attempting to stop the insanity of what's going on with university administrators not giving students due process constitutional protections.

Renee: I also think we can start by educating those, usually females are the accusers, educating them on taking responsibility for their own behavior. Regret doesn't equal rape and I really think helping them feel certainly supported but also take responsibility for their actions. I really feel strongly and I don't know how this would come across with universities, but there is a lot of drinking on campus and that gets a lot of people in trouble. A lot of these campuses consider themselves wet campuses; they turn their eye away to the amount of alcohol that students drink to just drink. I think a lot of education in rolling that back is going to be important.

Gary: Unfortunately, I think we live in a society where those that make accusations like this knowing they're not true have this belief, and somewhat I think they may be right, that there's no repercussions or accountability for what you do.

That's why I think false accusations have to be addressed. You file a false claim; they can charge you with a crime for that.

I think accountability is what's missing here. If your son came to you and your husband earlier and you found out about this, would you have made the assumption? See that's where I was totally naïve, I made the assumption that all of these went to a local police authority and that wasn't the case and that's what got me totally interested and involved with this.

Yeah, in my son's case not even the campus police got involved. We did hire a criminal attorney in the state that my son was in, if you're sentenced to rape, it's ultimately life in prison without parole.

Renee:

So it was a big deal. Again, we were learning through this process, learning as we went along.

One thing I wanted to say too about that phone call we received or if you have a son or daughter who is accused, is there may be some listeners who are thinking, "Well, she's his mom. Of course she's going to believe her son." But really what I want to say is just like I'm asking university administrators to do for the students, I had to ask myself regarding my son's case.

I had to listen really closely to my son tell me what happened. I had to ask a lot of detailed questions around the sexual interaction that are pretty uncomfortable for a 19-year old to share with his mom and see and read the evidence in the report for myself too.

But after doing all that, and looking at the private investigator work et cetera, there was enough evidence for me to 100% believe that my son absolutely did not do what he was accused of and certainly had a very unfair experience by his university administrators.

I just really feel strongly that there has to be some fairness to the process because right now the narrative from the opposing side is that these new guidelines they're dangerous, they're going to roll back protections for survivors, they're going to attempt to silence survivors, that there's an epidemic of sexual harassment, that Betsy DeVos needs to do more not less to ensure safety.

How I really would ask them to look at this process is let's go back to the Supreme Court decisions that has given basis for these new proposed guidelines and think about giving that fairness and due process to all students on that college campus.

Right now the cards are stacked more on the accuser's side and the new proposed guidelines from the Department of Education doesn't really take away cards from the accusers, rather it gives an equally stacked deck of cards to the accused.

Gary: To the accused, yeah.

Renee: Only when both sides have an equally stacked deck of cards can there be a fairer process.

These regulations clearly rest on Supreme Court decisions, law professor's statements, and judicial decisions. That's the place to start when trying to get more sanity back onto our college campuses.

Gary: Those that do not like the new laws or the way she has come across, narrowing the definition of sexual misconduct. I'm not sure that's really taking place. You hit the nail on the head when you're saying it's giving the accused the ability to defend themselves.

If that's how they define narrowing the definition, well so be it. Honestly, maybe I'm old-fashioned whatever, but I just don't believe that anybody but law enforcement should be at some point taking this case over if someone is accused of these types of crimes. Especially, Renee when you were telling me in the state that your son was in, it's life imprisonment. This is not joking around.

The way they're conducting these hearings and sending you stuff through emails and you're walking in and not being told that this is your one and only time to defend yourself, hence no preparation, that's even more disturbing.

Renee:

Right, yeah it is. And that's what these new guidelines are supposed to be stopping. But having cross-examinations is crucial for a fair system. It's called the greatest legal engine ever invented for the discovery of truth. Also, I'll just say one other point in the guidelines is that the school has the opportunity to allow mediation between the two students.

In my son's case that may very well have been a way to have combated this. They weren't allowed in the 2011 Obama Administration guidelines. The reason I say that is because after my son was expelled and he went in a tailspin downward for a while, just the trauma. About three months after he was expelled, he noticed on his LinkedIn account that his accuser had been looking into his account so he took that opportunity to email her back and ask her, "Why did you lie? Why did you say what you did when we both know it's not true?" He said, "I think I understand why the school did but I don't understand why you did and I've lost so much because of this."

She emailed him back within hours, really long email. And she said no less than 30 times she was sorry, "I'm sorry. I didn't mean it to get as far as it did." So again, what she originally went to the school for, like Trent said, he'd be speculative exactly why she said what she did, but we do think it stems from either regret or embarrassment or trying to protect her reputation.

When she went to the school, how we understand it is she didn't really say that he sexually assaulted her, she just said it was aggressive sexual interaction which she was very much a part of if that's the case. But the school took the ball and rolled with it so by the time it was all said and done, what my son was told in that first 30-minute, and only 30-minute, conversation was apparently aggressive sex, it turned into sexual assault. He didn't even know-

Gary: What was coming.

Renee: What he was expelled for wasn't even what he was ever told. That's what these new guidelines hopefully will correct.

Gary: All well and good but when you hear someone sending a long email apologizing. As you're telling me this I'm thinking to myself, "But still, what made you go to them to begin with?" I think alcohol, a little more counseling with these kids that are out of the home for the first time in regard to getting into these situations, I think maybe more needs to be done with that. Alcohol I think is a big problem and leads to a lot of these things but unfortunately the apology at the end is not good enough for me for your family. The damage to you, your family, your poor son, it's over. The damage has been done. I'm glad there's some new rulings and I'm glad some new guidelines. I debated someone yesterday on some of these and they were trying to tell me that I was not concerned about sexual assault victims. That's far from the truth. People will do that when they don't have the facts or understand what they're really talking about. I'm concerned about the accused, Renee because I want them to have all their rights, I want them to go through a process that will determine guilt or innocent and everybody walks away at that point. Not to be falsely accused, found guilty before their hearing even starts.

Renee: Right, I agree and I think just to comment on one of the questions you had, why did she even go originally to the student conduct office? I think one of the reasons is these accusers they speak with their friends, tell a lie, and they get pressure from their friends, "You need to do something." So that ultimately I think in her case is why she ended up going is because she had told a story to her friend and it just snowballed. Again, a small lie can grow into a big lie to where somebody's life is completely-

Gary: Renee we're at the top of the hour, if someone wanted to get a hold of you and talk to you, is there a way they can get a hold of you.

Renee: My email, I probably wouldn't want to give that right now. Probably-

Gary: Okay, if you give it to my producer when we get through the conversation then I'll have it if somebody does call and I'll determine at that point. But I appreciate you calling. I'm sorry that your family had to go through this but hopefully you'll institute some new change as we go forward.

Renee: Yeah, we're working for that. Well thank you for having me on Gary, I appreciate it.

Gary: You're welcome.

19

DAN PERKINS

Gary: On the line with us now is Dan Perkins, Dan is a master storyteller and author of the Brotherhood of the Red Nile, which centers around Islamic nuclear terrorism against the United States. He's also the author of some children's books, he's a nationally recognized expert on radical Islam and he contributed to the dailycaller.com, clashdaily.com, lifeset.com, newsmax.com and thehill.com. Dan, when's the new book coming out, or is it out yet?

Dan: No, the fourth book in the..

Gary: Trilogy, yeah.

Dan: If you can do such a thing, a fourth book in a trilogy, came out in January. And that's Ted Baker in search of terrorist's gold. That particular book was actually forced upon be because the people who finished the trilogy said, you can't do this to us. You can't leave us hanging here.

Gary: Right, right.

Dan: They are our family members and that's why I wrote the Terrorist Gold, but what's interesting about Terrorist Gold is that much like the first book in the trilogy, Sarah's perspective was written in, started in February of 2012. It's a story about a new terrorist group formed in central Syria in the town of Homs, who has a strategic relationship with the Iranian nuclear program, and they convert two old Soviet

Union suitcase dirty bombs into weapons of mass destruction and bring them into the United States.

Why that's important is that several years later a new terrorist organization called Isis was formed in the city of Homs, Syria. So not to be outdone Terrorist Gold, which was started in the summer of 2015, is the story about Russians getting control of a democratic nominee for president in the presidential election, and again in summer of 2015, long before anybody has actually become candidates for the president. So, a little bit prophetic.

Gary: Well I think all your books are little bit prophetic in that regard, because when I've read them, it's like, holy cow, this is like crazy. I'm looking, is this fiction or nonfiction this book? It was happening around us, that was the part that really made me get into that book and then read your other books, because it like unbelievable. And I've given your books to friends to read, Dan, and they all say the same the thing. And they all ask me on a regular basis, has he come out with a new book yet? I said, I'll be speaking with him this week and I'll find out.

Dan: Actually I'm working, so I started out writing Terrorist, and while I was concurrently writing Terrorist, I started writing children's books. A new genre for me.

Gary: Right.

Dan: And now I'm in the process of about 120 chapters into another pivot into historical fiction.

Gary: Really?

Dan: And this particular book is called Abraham Lincoln and the Second Assassin interesting title.

Gary:

Yeah, very interesting. Very interesting. So I want to just change the topic a little bit and talk to you about South Africa.

Dan:

Yes, sir.

Gary:

I have been following this the last month in detail; I listen to some overseas radio stations. I have been in touch with a gentleman from South Africa, who I'm trying to get on the air to interview, who's a farmer. The problem with interviews in South Africa is they lose electricity, and they use internet, and as I was telling Ted, my producer, earlier, 20-minute segment, we may be sitting here for two hours back and forth with him. But what you would say it's a systematic purge of white people taking place in South Africa. And that is the truth, Dan.

Dan:

But, Gary, that's true, and we can talk about that, and we should talk about that. But you inadvertently, I don't think you realize what you've done, is that you've really uncovered the real issue. The real issue isn't about, in my opinion based on what I've seen and people I've talked to, it's not about the farmers. It's not about reparation for blacks who had their lands stolen from. What it's about is keeping the lights on 24 hours a day. Why, because the coal that's under the land. There's a farmer there who has a game preserve that they found huge deposits of coal, and the government, the ANC's coming in and said, we're gonna take your land. And we might pay you 10 cents on the dollar, or we just may take it. And we have to decide. But they physically sent in geologists to go in do core samples and found there's a huge coal deposit.

The problem in South Africa, and many other of the African nations, is a lack of source of reliable power. And so South Africa is very rich in coal deposits and they haven't done a great job of necessarily identifying many of them, or if they find them to effective harvest the coal. And so what you have here, yes, you have an issue of the government telling them that they want the farms for reparation to blacks who the land was taken from, but in reality what's going on is they want the resources, the government wants the natural resources to exploit so that they can improve the economy of the country.

Ted: Dan, isn't this compound, I'm sorry, this is Ted, the producer. Isn't this problem with the coal compounded by their diamond issue?

Dan: You're absolutely right. If you're saying that the Europeans came in and developed the diamond mines and took the diamonds away from the Africans and gave them very little money for the diamonds or for the land. True. But what I'm talking about is something totally different. I'm talking about...

Ted: But don't they find a lot of diamonds in the coal?

Dan: Oh, there is a relative relationship; diamonds are basically coal that's been compressed for thousands of years. Yes, but the coal that was found as a result of the diamond exploration was a throwaway item, they really didn't use it. They were more interest in the value of the diamonds than the value of the coal. But as that economy across all of Africa is trying to becoming on the world stage as competing, their biggest problem is a reliable source of electrical power.

And there isn't the resources, the money to build massive solar power plants or wind plants because they're a poor nation. So this other gold in the ground, this coal now is becoming reality of a way in which the countries can begin to establish a reliable source of power. And with a reliable source of power you can have economic expansion.

Gary: You know, Dan, there's no doubt about it to me that the motivation of the government is to get at the coal, and they're going through the process of, you know, we're gonna take the land, and we're gonna give it to black individuals to farm. And shortly thereafter, pretty soon they'll be mining these lands, we all know that. And there's a couple of issues there, because when you look at it, and we talked about this a little earlier on the show, you just don't hand someone the keys to a farm and say, now you're a farmer, you're gonna produce food for millions of people. That just doesn't happen. So, that's why right away I was very suspicious of what was going on with these land takeovers.

But the other side of this, that's all well and good, they have a great resource under the ground, and they're gonna probably eliminate numerous farmers, or even as they shut them down with this façade that we're trying to give back land to the black people. Sooner or later they're gonna be faced with the problem of no food. When you start eliminating farms that are producing the food for your populous, you have a serious problem when they start closing and falling apart.

Dan: And a part of the challenge here, Gary, is that the Afrikaners, who own the majority of the farmland, had already had a program in effect for years because of what you said, the fact that the blacks don't know anything about farming and turning the land over to them is not going to help them. They started a cooperative situation where they would bring in black on their farms, they would pay them a wage, but they would teach them how to farm, run the equipment, take care of livestock. And in some cases after some period of time, would allow them to buy some of the land of the farm and establish their own farm.

Gary: Right.

Dan: But you're absolutely right, if you don't know how to turn on a tractor, how are you ever going to maintain a tractor, or a plow or whatever, or take care of the herd of cows, whatever's there. If you have no experience in doing that, just because the government gives you the deed to the property doesn't mean that they're gonna know how to farm.

               Now the problem I have, Gary, with what's going on is the incredible misinformation that's coming out. Just to give you two examples.

Gary: Hold that thought, Dan, we're gonna take a quick break. You're listening to Business, Politics and Lifestyles, my name is Gary Goldman.

               On the line with us now is author Dan Perkins. Dan, I've got to ask you, you know there's a lot of violence going on, violent crimes and violent acts to farmers, and when I was talking to this individual in South Africa via email, my question was, who's sending these thugs in? Is it the government to try and scare you off your land, or is it someone else? I'm still trying to figure it out, because they're going in to some of these farms and obviously killing off family members and farmers, and I'm like, if they're trying to change the ownership of the farms, that's not actually the right way to do it. You want to sort of keep these people around to help you get going. Then I started to say, with the resources and knowing what's under the ground, maybe it's the government sending these people in to scare them off their land.

Dan: Well that's a great question, because that's one of the things I was going to talk about just before the break and that is the enormous about of misinformation. For example, there are newspapers outside the United States and online bloggers who are characterizing this as a genocide. Now, I am not in any way diminishing the value of human life, but depending upon who you read you can find out in 2017 there were between 47 and 65 white farmers that were killed in 2017. Pretty wide disparity. So I have a hard time calling it genocide. I have also read both sides of the story. I've read that the government is bringing in the thugs and I heard or is the opposition party is bringing in the thugs, and they're the ones that are pushing for this change in the constitution that allows the government to come in and just take your land and not pay you anything for it at all.

But what I was saying is that the white Afrikaners realizing the issue of the lack of ability of a lot of black Africans to be able to successfully run farms, they started in essence an apprentice program where those who wanted to learn how to farm could come and work with them and work on their farms, be taught how to run the machinery and take care of animals and everything else. And then when they finish their apprenticeship they were able to go out and buy a land to start their own farm, or they bought land from the farmer that they were working for. So there was a solution in the works to try and bring the parties together in amenable way that dealt with some of the issues.

But when you hire thugs to go in and kill the farmers and rape the wives and daughters, and you got farmers the last number I saw, again if you can believe the number, about 15000 Afrikaners went to the Soviet Union where they were welcomed and were given rights to land to establish farms there. So, it is a very disruptive situation.

It's also interesting, Gary, when you reverse the transaction, when whites in the United States kill blacks it's considered to be racist. But they don't report it being racist when blacks in South Africa kill whites.

Gary: Right.

Dan: So it's a kind of a double standard here. And by and large the administrations of the last two presidents, although the president has been looking into this situation, trying to get as much information as possible. Clearly Obama before he left was very much in favor of the ANC government and what they were trying to do. So it's a difficult problem, but the one issue that I really think is important that I have yet to see anybody write anything extensively about is this issue about what do they do about the mineral rights and more specifically the coal.

And I think that's not being talked about. I think it's not being talked about purposefully. I think the government doesn't want to tell the people that really, really what they want is to take the land and take out the coal to build power plants and try and improve the economy, which is admirable but to steal the land, you know, it's interesting we have going on in our country a similar situation. And I've written about this. What we basically have is the opposition party sees themselves as a socialist party.

Gary: Yep.

Dan: They want to take the land, give it to the government and let the government decide who's gonna get and how they're gonna get it. Well, what they're talking about is the socialist manifesto, which is really close to communism, and what we have is Ms. Cortez up in New England, in New York City, who is an avowed socialist running under the democratic banner. And she wants to do the same thing. She wants to take and she wants to give everybody free health insurance, free Medicare, free college, guaranteed income as a federal employee, and she wants to take the money from corporations, not taxes, she wants to take their profit and she wants to acquire our portfolios as individuals to take that money and the income to pay for all these socialist programs.

And it's interesting when you look at the socialist mentality, they always, the next generation of socialist always believe that they've got the key, they can make it work. It may not have worked before but they'll say, they were doing it wrong, we have the right way to do it. And I don't believe they do.

The other thing is, in the last 100 years, if you look at the socialist countries around the world, 100 million people have been murdered under socialist leadership in the last 100 years. It doesn't work. So Cortez is the American in what's going on in Africa.

Gary: And when you talk about the new socialists, they like to refer to themselves as the democratic socialists, they think by putting that word democratic in there it's gonna soften the tone. And Cortez, she's an interesting individual, I personally think there's a lot more for her.... those with her perspective sitting in the wings, maybe an elected office right now, and they're just they're waiting for the opportunity to come out and talk in the same manner she has. Not to get off track, but listening to her talk and her ideas and not having any insight into how things really operate is scary, it's just totally scary. It's one thing to have a thought process, Dan, but to not understand what you're opposing is even scarier.

Ted: And without rebuff capitalism there are no social programs.

Gary: Right, right.

Dan:

Right, right. And you're looking at, going back to Africa again, the issue really is, Gary, is that the socialist do not think about the unintended or intended consequences of their actions. They're not thinking about, okay, if we take the land, and we can get the coal, are we gonna have the money to build the power plants? And if we're gonna build the power plants, are we going to comply with the Paris accord, or are we gonna say screw the Paris accord, we're gonna generate power?

Rolling blackouts is a very common thing in Africa because there's not a reliable source of power to meet the demands of the people of South Africa and other African nations. And so, like the socialists, I don't think they're thinking far enough ahead, once they take the land and once they start to extract the coal, what are they gonna do with it? And you need a lot of money to build power plants. A lot of money to build power plants. And if you've got a socialist nation it's gonna be hard to attract Western capital to come in and try and build power plants.

Gary:

Especially with the narratives that investors are hearing as to what's going on, because overall, not a safe place to be. You talk to, or you read about people who live there and they pull into their houses, they put their garage door up for example, they put it down, they keep their cars locked, the garage is like a safe room before they even get into their homes. So this is just one of many issues going on over there, so whether there's a vast amount of coal, that's great, but getting, as you say, investors to come in there and spend their money may be difficult.

Dan:

Right. Absolutely correct.

Gary:

Dan, how can people find you and get ahold of you?

Dan: Danperkins.guru is the website, we're in the process of
            updating it and making it even more efficient, but you'll see
            everything there from books to radio interviews like yours, to
            television, international television, commentary and songs
            and stories for soldiers all on one place. So we hope to get it
            finished within the next week to 10 days, it's gonna be
            spectacular.

Gary: Great. And keep me informed of the new book when we
            should expect that, and as usually, great having you on the
            show and look forward to speaking with you again soon,
            Dan.

Dan: Any time. Thank you for having me, have a great weekend.

20

PAULA WHITE

Gary: But we do have our next guest on the line, pastor Paula White. Paula is the personal minister and spiritual advisor to President Donald Trump. She's the author of the book, Dare to Dream: Understand God's Design For Your Life. Good morning and welcome to the show.

Paula: Good Morning Gary. I pray you're doing well and all your listeners. And it's good to be with you this morning.

Gary: It's great to have you on. So, yeah. I was talking about that horrific scene in California last week and, when I read that gunman's Facebook little rant that he put on there, to me it was a cry for help. And I think, as a society, we really need to start dealing with the real problems at hand, as opposed to some of the offshoots of the problem. Guns can be a problem, but there's more to the stories and these shootings than just guns, pastor. It's very sad. Lives and communities are ruined. Pittsburgh, two weeks ago, California the other day, part of California, it's horrible.

Paula: I couldn't agree with you more, Gary. As a pastor for 23 years, I work with a dear friend, Dr. Tim Clinton of the American Association of Christian Counselors that has over 50 thousand mental health care counselors, providers, etc. And, on a daily basis, in ministry, obviously, your life is connecting people and connecting God. And so, I see that the root of the problem, and grateful that this administration understands the epidemic, and has done so much through HHS, through the opioid crisis, through so many different things to understand that we have to help people. And much of that help, I mean our VA, all that's taking place through the Veterans Peer Program, and some of the programs our president has created along with the department to really get to the root.

And people need help. Our society is different than 50 years ago. It's completely different thing. And I personally, my story, Gary, is I didn't grow up in church. I kind of radically had this revolution when I was 18 years old. But really we all have drivers in our life. And my father, when I was five years old, took his life. So, I understand how people can make really desperate decisions. It would be years later that we would find out that he was seeing somebody, God only knows what they had him on. And so, it's a personal place of passion for me to help people, to get them the right care.

Prayer does a lot. We know that prayer changes things. I know that our faith is absolutely vital, and sometimes people need those tools, skills, and their medication. And getting them the right help is extremely vital.

Gary: Yeah, it's not like one size fits all. And I hate to make it sound so simple. There is a number of things that are involved in helping people. And a lot of people say, that's what's missing. People, if they don't have something to believe in, that's a big part of the equation that's missing that can be very difficult within their lives. They may not even know it, pastor. They might not even know that's part of it. And that makes it even sadder, when you think of that situation.

Paula: So true. The entire Gospel, and hope, and message of Jesus Christ talks and he came to seek and save that which was lost, which really translates into, he came to put back into position that which was mispositioned. I think life has a way of getting us out of position sometimes that we don't even know. We don't understand why are we so empty? Why are we beneath that baseline? What pushed us under that threshold? And when, someone just shares, they don't have to beat you over the head with the Bible, just shares their life, their love, and the radiance, the light of God, and that's what, as believers and Christians, we're called to do.

I think that our president, that was a deep, I want to say, point of attraction for him. The way that we met 18 years ago, he was watching Christian television. And I came to find out he admired and loved Dr. Billy Graham, and David Jeremiah, and so many. And, as the self-made man that was very successful, I can picture as a pastor what it was like for him to go to church. Most people were more struck with his celebrityship at that time, whereas I was like, just this is a man that needs God like all of us.

And so, that was a point of connection that we really connected. He called me up out of the blue and repeated to me, actually, three of my sermons that he'd been watching, and repeated them verbatim.

Gary: Wow.

Paula: On value of vision. And that's like, Gary, I was like, wow. He's listening better than most of my congregation. And he started telling me stories about how he was confirmed Presbyterian and grew up in Norman Hills, and began to share with me some sermons that had really impacted his life, how his father would take him to Dr. Billy Graham's Crusade, and how important his faith was to him.

And he was, at times, I mean, I never actually shared this publicly, but challenged when he'd go to church, he simply wanted to worship God. He really wanted to make connection and hear the word God. And sometimes not, like all places in our society and human beings can be, we can get in awe of something or have a wrong motive, or want something of someone that we think or perceive has value. And so, part of his being fed daily with his faith was he would watch Christian television, listen to Christian music.

And that's how, 18 years ago, that relationship began. I'm grateful that I get to serve. And I love to think of it as, not only being spiritual advisor to him and the family and much of an administration, and this goes way back. I mean, from our president to, Ivanka, and Don Jr., and Eric, and Laura, and Jared, and First Lady Melania, and then of course, many staff members at Trump organizations, we all became very close in the capacity that I've been able to walk with this family and his friends.

And so, now, like I said, in the White House, I like to think of it as the heart and soul of the White House. So, we work on issues that are so important. I spent much of yesterday doing prison reform, and working on situations with immigration, and alleviating poverty. Many people don't talk about the 3 million people, statistics from months ago, that came off of food stamps and welfare. And I wrote an op-ed one time, or a few, I think, that I just said, the EO you've never heard of.

Gary: Right.

Paula: It was an executive order he signed on alleviating poverty. And I looked at it immediately and it was like nine principles, and I don't have it right in front of me here, but I think it's nine or something, and it was just boom, boom, boom. I went, well, that's what God's words says. You know, it's nine biblical principles. And I said, if you do this, of course you're going to alleviate. It's following the creator's instruction, the one who is the wisest and knows the best. And it's amazing that he continues to walk in his steps. And those are the things that get so overlooked.

Gary: Yeah. And that's the frustration. Because, I mean, you know the president from a whole different side. And the media wants us to believe he's not the person that you know. But there's so much out there, things like you are telling us that he does, all the good things that's just being overlooked. And it's so shameful because he's doing it for the country. I personally believe that President Trump really believes that, when people talk about, make America great again, that's just not some slogan to him. That's him. That's what he really feels.

Paula: Absolutely.

Gary: And we're led to believe it's some political slogan that he just happened to stumble across, and that's not the case. And that must frustrate you when you hear some of the stuff that you hear or see, or the lack of conversation on the things that he's doing.

Paula: It is frustrating, Gary, because, as you said, I do have a different perspective. I've known him and his family for 18 years and I'm in the bowel and the heart of everything. And so, I get to see. I can tell you story, after story, after story. It's easier for me to interpret some of his actions and his words and etc. But the media and some of the likes I've never seen, I mean, just the disrespect and criticism towards the office of anybody.

Gary: Yeah. That's very, very frustrating.

Paula: It is unbelievable. And you're absolutely right. I mean, when you think about it just from a common sense, practical standpoint, this is a man who did not need anything. I mean, very successful with multi billions, incredible family, you've heard it out of his own mouth. Talk about, I've kind of pretty much been successful and happy. Right? I've had a good life, he says. I've had a good life. And he has had an extremely good life.

And I saw some meme or something on one of the social medias that said, works for free, gets up and is the hardest working president, etc., every single day. Battles through just battle after battle, has put at stake his businesses, his family, and everything else with absolutely everything to lose and nothing to gain. And why does he do it? Because he does believe that God has called him to make America great. I believe, emphatically, that the Lord has to put him in that position, and the Psalms simply says, God raises one up, puts another down. Promotion comes from not the south, east, or the west are from the Lord. There's a lot of his history.

His mother was a very, very strong woman, a strong Christian. There's a lot of lineage and legacy there from his great, great aunts, great cousin who were a big part of this Scottish revival. I said, when we look at people, it's not like they just came out of nowhere. He didn't just say, well, one day I'm going to be president.

Gary: Right.

Paula: I think he saw that the nation that he grew up in, the opportunities that his father seized, his family afforded, what hard work and opportunity can bring forth, I think he saw the crumbling of that, religious liberties, the crumbling of that. So many things that were important in our security, our borders, our military. Maybe people do know, some don't know his background. And if you understand a person's background patterns people tend to focus on, all of us have an Achilles heel, or a weakness, or an area of vulnerability, and all of us have strengths and things that we've done. And it certainly seems, with this president, they focus on just whatever went wrong, never the patterns of everything in his life. Like he did go off military school, why that is so important in his understanding. Of course, we know him as a financial business person.

What maybe some people don't know is what an incredible history buff he is. He knows history, and cycles, and understands things, and, not only understands America, understands the world. These are conversations way before consideration of presidency.

Gary: In... oh. Go ahead. I'm sorry.

Paula: Go ahead, Gary. I could go on and on forever, because I could tell those stories. I could tell his compassionate side. I could tell the times that I've watched him just send his jet to pull a young girl that had cancer or leukemia, can't remember what the exact disease was. And insurance was not there. She needed a transplant with something they wouldn't get her from the state. And so, for this last ditch effort, the parents just randomly called Trump Towers and he was like, send my jet. It wasn't call my attorneys and the interns, just send it. Get her.

I mean, and I could tell you whether it was a person that we walked down the street. I have a place in New York, and he would often leave this place, and he always walked out of his way and would go up to the construction workers. They were like, hey, Trump. And he'd go over and talk to them, how is the building going. And it wasn't his building. It'd be something else.

I'll do one more, and then I'll-

Gary: No, no. That's fine.

Paula: His yes is his yes and his no is his no. And I remember going in his office one time, and it was a very big situation, it would become a very big deal for him. But, at the time, if somebody came and pitched something to him and he really liked it, thought it was a good deal, he would just say, yes. I'll do it. Now, it wasn't like he was getting paid a ton of money. He shook his hand and said yes. And then he proceeded afterwards; he called his agent, called his attorneys and said, hey. I'm going to be doing this. And they could, absolutely not. It's a career killer. You don't do this. It doesn't fit you. It's not going to be right. And his response to them was, but I shook his hand. And that was the end of it for him. But I shook his hand. So, it was, I'm doing this because I told him and I shook his hand.

And I know that to be the person. I could, again, keep going. I remember one time rarely, I would spend hours and hours up in his office, just if I was in town. I lived in New York, had a church in New York, and did a Bible study for the New York Yankees. And he and Austin, or Rhona, or Keith, or somebody would call me up, or one of the kids, and say, you're in town? Why don't you stop by? I'd stay ten minutes and it would end up being hours. And I'd sit there in his office like a fly on the wall thinking I'm going to be kicked out of this meeting. But I was there.

And there was a day, I rarely took people up, but I would take some of my friends. And they would say, we want to meet Mr. Trump or whatever. And we're looking way back, years ago. And I took two of my girlfriends that were there, and one of them happened to be the daughter of a very, very high profile ministry passed along. Her brother has probably one of the largest churches in the nation. And I took her best friend who had been a dear friend of mine.

Obviously, Mr. Trump knew the person who had the very large ministry, and he was talking to them. And bursting in then he said, now what do you do, to the other girl, her name was Deborah. And she said, well, sir, I go out on the streets and I minister to prostitutes, and work with the homeless, and she began to go into her ministry, which is an absolute street ministry of ministering, especially to women, who have been battered, and are on the streets, and prostitution, an etc., and in strip clubs, and on, and on.

And he said, now, that's real ministry. And he goes, Rhona. And Rhona comes in and he says, boom, just right there writes out an extremely large check. And I thought to myself, that's the Trump I know, which by the way, I have never received a dime from Mr. Trump because I, when I met him, the Lord spoke to me and said, and this is never to minimize his faith or where he came from, but God spoke to me and said, show him who I am. And I knew that it was an assignment.

And so, early on, we laugh about it now, I went in about second meeting or third time, and I said sir, I don't want your money. I have enough of my own. I don't want your fame. I have enough of my own. I said, I want your soul. And I think I walked out, and I think he just thought I was crazy enough or something.

Gary: Well, that's all right. I mean-

Paula: Yeah.

Gary: But, well first of all, you're our in to get Donald Trump on the air sometime, but we won't go there right now. But the what bothers me when I have conversations with people and I say, let's put the politics aside and talk about who Donald Trump really is. And you start telling them things and they have a hard time believing it, because that's not what they're hearing all day. But what really frustrates me are these hypocrites, whether it's the main stream media or other politicians that used him, knew exactly who Donald Trump really is, were there to take his money, and now they're trying to make him out like he's a totally different person. I think that frustrates a lot of people, but it's not right.

You don't have to like his policy as president but don't rip apart who the man is. And that's what really bothers me.

Paula: I agree, Gary. And again, I recognize things in a different perspective, and I've watched it over and over, when we first went to early on, I mean, well back in 2011 and then I'll go to early on, he called and said, Paula, would you bring some pastors around and pray? I'm really thinking about running for president. And so, we did. And we prayed with him for six hours. I mean, I know pastors that don't pray for 60 minutes, you know?

Gary: Yep, yep.

Paula: And I mean, he would walk in and out, but predominantly, he was there. And six hours he prayed. And the next day I said, what do you believe God is saying, and I mean genuinely seeking. And it wasn't like, hey, get them around because I want a vote. Get them around because he never asked that. Even during the campaign, it wasn't, get these evangelicals to vote for me. He wanted to hear the heart of the community. He wanted to know what was going on. And yeah, I mean, he was the one that came up with it and went, you guys have lost the power of your voice. You can't even stand in your pulpits and speak what's on your heart for righteousness sake, and you can't endorse someone. And then, I would watch, when my husband John and I went with the kids and him up to one of his first speaking engagements early on in the campaign. And, in that rally, I would call it, it wasn't quite a rally yet, but in that engagement, then we watched it on TV. And, if I wasn't there and I was just watching TV, and it would only get worse, and it would only increase, and, if I had not been in those places myself and watched TV, I would be like, oh my goodness. It's just unbelievable because they were so distorted.

Gary: Right.

Paula: So wrong. In the rallies I would watch, initially the first few rallies that we were a part of and went to and I would speak, or open, or he would always Paula, would you please come pray for is, etc. And we'd watch this sudden disruption, and he looked at me like, these are kids that are paid. When you do that enough, it starts creating chaos. Create enough chaos and you end up with some of where we are today. And that was not President Trump. He didn't do that.

What I saw was what people saw in the Missouri rally that broke out in Amazing Grace. I saw a man that, if a person would pass out, he'd have three rallies or so back to back, and exhausting himself, and he'd stop everything and he'd wait. And I remember one rally, a lady had fainted and he stopped for over an hour to make sure she was okay. He always usually whispers over to me and say, Paula, go pray for her, or send someone down and make sure the paramedics took care of her. And he would just stop everything. The cameras never showed that.

Gary: No, they never showed. Because I covered him when he-

Paula: So-

Gary: Came here to Massachusetts, when he was in Wooster. And seeing was believing because the media had a whole different perspective. There was one protester, a few protesters; they were trying to make that as the issue. And when you heard him speak, and you saw the groups of people there, you know that he was for real. Paula, we're at the top of the hour. How can people find you or get your book?

Paula: Go to www.PaulaWhite.org. The website is the best way. And I'd love them to follow me on social media. Of course, it's the blue check on, and that's Paula White. I use my name Paula White Cain, but Paula White, the real Paula White. So, just the easiest way is go to the website, and that's PaulaWhite.org. And I'd love to just connect with them. I talk a lot about some of the events, and how they can get involved, and people that would love to be involved. We just had 250 people up at the Department of Education yesterday getting briefings on everything. And I'd love to host the listening sessions and be a part of that. So, people can be much more involved than I think they realize. They don't have to just watch on TV, they can actually go to the White house, because the president has opened the doors to people to be very involved.

Gary: Well, the next time you have the president, it's okay to tell him about our show. We'd love to have him on there.

Paula: He's got it, Gary. I'll do it.

Gary: Yeah. And thank you for your time, and I have been on your sites, and they're all great stuff. And I'll keep in touch and I look forward to speaking with you again as time goes on.

Paula: Thank you. Many blessings to you, and happy Saturday.

Gary: Thank you. You too.

21

DR. WARREN FARRELL

Gary: On the line with us now is Dr. Warren Farrell. Dr. Farrell is the author of The Boy Crisis: Why Our Boys Are Struggling and What Can We Do About It? Dr. Farrell is currently the chair of the commission to create a White House council on boys and men. Good morning Dr. Farrell, and welcome to the show.

Warren Farrell: Good morning. I'm looking forward to talking with you.

Gary: So I went through your book very interesting, and talking to a lot of people yesterday. I was talking to friends of mine and about this title. Based on the events that happened last Sunday, during that gaming event, and it's funny people's opinion when you get into a topic like this, they either want to shun it off and not believe some of the things we're going to talk about are happening, or they're very much interested, and have very different opinion, what is going on with the male role in the household in the United States of America.

Warren Farrell: You are absolutely correct. I find that to be very much true. I do find that teachers are pretty unanimous in seeing, especially elementary, secondary school teachers, are pretty unanimous in seeing that there's this big gap between boys and girls in their school, and they don't really know what it's about. And there's a lot of reasons it exists, but they have a lot of different opinions as to why. And certainly, when there's, you have David Katz like last Sunday, he did the shooting in Florida after the gaming event, and the response is, "Well, you know, that's the violence and video games, or that's the violence in the media as a whole, or that's the poor family values, or that's access to guns, or that's mental illness." And each of them is a player, by the way.

Warren Farrell: But our daughters live in the same homes with the same family values, the same access to the same guns, the same video games, the same media, and similar overlapping mental illnesses. And our daughters are not doing the killing, and our sons are. This is the issue that fascinated me, that got me to do the research for The Boy Crisis. Like, what is this about? And my first real hint was seeing that in all 63 of the largest developed countries, the test administered by the UN, an outlet of the UN, indicated that boys were falling behind girls in every single academic subject. It used to be boys were at least ahead of girls in math and science. Now they are about, a little bit behind girls in math and science, but considerably behind girls in reading and writing. And it's reading and writing that are the two biggest predictors of success.

Warren Farrell: So I started asking myself, what do these 63 nations have in common? And what they have in common is that they are the largest developed nations. I was asking then what do developed nations have in common, and two of the things that they have in common is much more permission for divorce, because they're not so preoccupied with survival, and much more permission for women to be able to have children without having father involvement. So I started looking at the data from that perspective, and started looking and realizing that there was this huge gap between boys who had significant father involvement. Those boys were doing extremely well, versus boys that did not have significant father involvement. Then I started looking at the numbers there. And in the United States, 53% of women under 30 who have children have them without being married. Now sometimes this means the father is barely known. Sometimes the father doesn't even know that he has a child. Other times the father is living with the mother, and the assumption is that that will be as good as being married. But on average, the mother and father who are living together when they have a child, the child and the father only remained connected for about three to four years. Now this is devastating for the girl, but it's much more devastating for the boy because the boy has no role model. The culture has giving girls a sense of purpose in the last 20, 30 years. They can raise children or they can raise money or they can do some combination of both.

Warren Farrell: But the old sense of purpose that boys used to have, be a warrior or a sole breadwinner, is no longer as strong. So you have this purpose void for boys, combined with a dad void. And those two together seem to leave boys without purpose, and without what dads bring to the family. And so I started asking myself, well, what do dads bring to the family that's leading to children who don't have fathers to do worse in 70 different areas? And the most important thing that dads tend to bring to the family that is different than mom style parenting is this willingness to do boundary enforcement, and this willingness to bond with the children through rough housing, and the willingness to get their sons to deal with things that are uncomfortable to them, and deal with stress effectively. So that's what I started to look at, was this difference between dad style parenting and mom style parenting that led to boys doing so well when they had that combination and so poorly when they don't.

Gary: You know, doctor, when you talk with people about these types of statistics, right away, a lot of people immediately when I've had discussions with them, will discount it, "Well, it's a discipline problem." Maybe a discipline problem, but they're not dealing with it based on the facts that you outlined, which is that old kicking the can down the road adage. There's a problem, we don't really know what it is, we just keep moving it along. Which is why it perpetuates. It becomes even worse.

Warren Farrell: Yes. And then, so if they say it's a discipline problem, actually you can pick up and say, "A lot of it is." So let's look at what there is about dad style parenting and mom style parenting that leads to a greater amount of discipline in dad style parenting. So for example, if, especially after a divorce, this is true, but it's true in general. Say the child is having dinner. Mom and dad will do the exact same boundary setting. They'll both say, "Sweetie, you could have ice cream. We have ice cream for dessert. You can have it as soon as you finish your peas." With the mom, and the child will test the boundaries of course with those parents to see how few peas she or he could eat before they have the ice cream.

Warren Farrell: And mom's response, especially after divorce, she's feeling guilty that there's a divorce, she's feeling the child's stress, she's sympathetic to the child's stress. And the child says, "I want the ice cream now." And Mom will tend to say something like, "Well sweetie, I said you couldn't have your ice cream until you finish your peas. But I'll tell you what. If you have a few more peas, then you can have your ice cream." And the mom is thinking in the back of your mind, it's a stressful day, we've had a divorce, or even if she hasn't had a divorce, maybe the child didn't do well in school, felt badly in school, was bullied at school. The mom was just saying, "We don't have very many precious moments together, so I don't want to go ahead and make a big argument over a few peas. That would be silly and insensitive."

And the dad's response is much more likely to be, "Excuse me, we have a deal here. The deal is that you can have your ice cream when you finish your peas, but you haven't finished your peas." "Well mom lets me have the ice cream when I have finished just a few more peas." "That's mom, I'm different. You must finish your peas before you have your ice cream." "You are so mean." "Well, you can continue crying and whining like that and then you'll have no ice cream tomorrow night either."

The boy's takeaway, or the girl's takeaway from this, is like with mom, I can manipulate a better deal.

Gary: Right.

Warren Farrell: So what the child focuses on is not the attention on finishing the peas, but the attention on what is there that mom is upset about or vulnerable to or that I can say that gives me a better deal. Whereas with dad, the child learns that I've got to focus on finishing my peas in order to get the ice cream. And that is the introduction to the child psychology of postponed gratification. And that's also the introduction of not getting ADHD. So for example, when children are raised by dads predominantly, only 15% have ADHD. When children are raised by moms predominantly, 30% have ADHD. And if you look at that example, you can see that with the mother, the child learns that I can manipulate the better deal and I don't have to focus my attention on finishing the peas. So she or he develops an attention deficit. With the father, the child develops attention focus and an attention discipline.

The difference is that the child with the father is far more likely to learn the single biggest predictor of success, which is postponed gratification, and learning that you can't have that ice cream until you do something that you don't really want to do, but you have to do. And so then that starts the slippery slope. And the slippery slope is that the child without postponed gratification doesn't finish the homework, doesn't rehearse for a school play or a sport that she or he is good at, but not great at, and wants to become, get on the varsity team, but doesn't have enough discipline to do that.

So then that child doesn't get the approval of, not only dad and mom feel a little bit disappointed in him, but he senses the disapproval of the teacher. Then when it becomes boy girl time, he sees that the girls don't go out with losers, the cheerleaders are cheering for the kids that risk their spinal cord injuries and concussions doing well in football, and so he starts feeling like he can't get women directly. So he starts turning to video games, video porn, or becoming addicted to video games to get some type of connection to a quick fix of dopamine. And both of those on the addiction level hurt his brain. Then that leads to alienation. He doesn't learn as good social skills in school. Boys with minimal amount of father involvement have much worse social skills, much less empathy.

Warren Farrell: Without the social skills and the empathy, that leads to fewer friendships and more temptation to go down the slippery slope into not just video game playing, which is perfectly fine, but a video game addiction, which is very harmful. And then also porn. And then that leads to depression, alienation, and in the worst case scenarios, suicide, or the mass shooting.

Gary: We're speaking with Dr. Warren Farrell, who is the author of the book, The Boy Crisis: Why Our Boys Are Struggling and What We Can Do About It. Dr. Farrell, we're going to take a short break. When we return, I want to talk to you about suicide and drugs given to these kids when they're, trying to control them when they're really not getting to the root of the problem.

Warren Farrell: Absolutely.

Gary: We are speaking with Dr. Warren Farrell, who's the author of
                        the book, The Boy Crisis: Why Our Boys Are Struggling and
                        What We Can Do About It.

                        You know, Dr. Farrell, when you talk about ADHD, and I
                        know children that have been diagnosed with this, there's a
                        tendency to put them on medication a lot of times, to
                        hopefully solve the problem. But when you look at that and
                        the more you study about this, this particular, if we want to
                        call it a disease, it's one thing to give child medication. But if
                        you're not dealing with the root of the problem, whether it's
                        the lack of the dad in the household, or even if the dad's
                        there, and the child becomes so manipulative he knows how
                        to play mom versus dad, that drug really isn't going to solve
                        that problem.

Warren Farrell: You're absolutely correct. In a sense, one of the antidotes to
                        ADHC is father involvement, but it also is a type of father
                        involvement. In their words if the father and the mother, if a
                        father is weak and does not say anything. And mom says,
                        "You're so mean because you forced the child to have the
                        peas when he's upset." And then the father realizes that the
                        only time I get approval from mom is when I get out of here
                        and I work hard and bring in money. And so, all right, I'll let
                        her take care of the children and I'll back off. Or, conversely,
                        sometimes you have a very weak dad and a very strong mom,
                        and the strong mom doesn't feel supported in her discipline
                        with the child. Then you're going to have problems.

                        One of the underlying causes of ADHD, aside from this
                        postponed gratification and the discipline that we were
                        talking about before is also to make sure that the child has
                        physical exercise. A significant amount of consistent physical
                        exercise every day for at least 20 to 30 minutes is very
                        important. And not baseball type of exercise where you're
                        standing in center field waiting for a call to eventually come.

But much more active, physical exercise. I think if baseball were invented today it probably would not be considered an exercise. That's very important too.

Gary: You know, and it's funny because I was watching a TV show the other night, and one of the children on it was diagnosed with ADHD. And the mother has a bottle of drugs, and they were talking about, no, the other family members didn't want to go that way. And then someone came up with the idea of he needs to burn off energy, and they had them start playing some hockey several hours a day. And it was amazing. Though it was a sitcom but told a great story. In a short period of time had better comments from the teachers, better reaction around the home.

Gary: So I Googled some of this last night and was reading different scenarios where physical exercise is the way to go. But Doctor, nowadays, there's this mentality. The way the world is, people are scared to let their kids out. They have to hover over them if they're out. Some parents consider physical exercise video gaming. I mean you need to get out, smell the fresh air, and do something that burns energy.

Warren Farrell: Yes. So if you're listening to Mr. Goldman and myself talk on this issue, this is not just speculation, this is really very good data behind the value of exercise. And also you slipped in something else there, which is being out in nature, and being out in nature is a very important antidote to ADHD. And let's also be clear here too. This is a real dilemma that parents have. They see that their child is not doing well, is not motivated, is not learning in school, is not focused. And they see some other neighbor as some other classmate has a parent who gives them drugs, and then that child is suddenly on Adderall and is doing better. And so there's such temptation, because you're afraid that your child is going to have in his early fundamental, foundational years of school, a bad attitude towards schools. So you want to fix that problem quickly. So that's understandable and I want to really empathize with that desire.

John Gray, my coauthor, wrote four chapters on alternatives to drugs. And there are so many alternatives in terms of healthier food. Sugar is another major contributor to ADHD. And also it is genetic, a genetic propensity to it versus not to it. So I mean, if your child has ADHD, it's usually because of a genetic propensity combined with a lifestyle, and the lifestyle thing needs to be addressed quickly. So if you're going to put your child on drugs, make sure you are following every other thing that you can do to counter that, and make sure that that drug is just a very short term crutch. But ideally try to follow the prescriptions of maybe more than 100 solutions that my co-author John Gray suggests to not have to put your child on drugs for ADHD. Drugs solve one problem. And every medical doctor will tell you almost any drug that's effective is effective by hurting other things that you also need in your system.

Gary: Yeah. And I think, you know, and I understand parents, you know, things can be difficult, working hard. But at some point when you decide to have a child, I don't want to get into that whole spiel, and you run into this situation, you have to be willing to put the time. And I think we've almost become a society where, problem, go to the doctor, go to the drug store and things are going to be okay. In this particular case it's not.

And another thing, you talk about boys without fathers growing up less involved and more likely to drop out of school, which you talked about, drink, do drugs, become delinquent, and end up in prison.   The last few days knowing you were coming on, I was doing some of this type of research, the numbers are astonishing, Doctor, that that cycle, the way that cycle exists.

Warren Farrell: It really is. Well first, let me deal with the first part of what you said, which is really important, and people really need to understand this. We often talk about there's, women should have the freedom to have children and raise the children by themselves and be single moms. And it is absolutely true. I was on the board of directors of the National Organization for Women in New York City for three years and spoke all around the world and the importance of the women's movement. And I bless it for the expansion of opportunities that gave women. And, at the same time, one of the flaws of the women's movement was talking about freedom for women to be able to raise children by themselves.

Warren Farrell: Yes, every woman should have the freedom to have children, but when she has children, you're making a free choice to sacrifice your freedoms oftentimes, in order to decide what is better for the children. And what is better for the children is being able to do your homework about learning communication with the father, and so the father and the mother look at what the differences are, the 10 major differences between dad style parenting and mom style parenting, and communicate about those differences. Dad is far more likely, for example, to be fine with rough housing, and mom is far more likely to look askance and see the father rough housing and saying, "Oh my god, this is just one more child I have to monitor."

Warren Farrell: But, almost no one understands why is it that rough housing leads to children being able to be more empathetic, less aggressive. These are very counter intuitive understandings, and almost no father that I know of knows how to explain these things to the moms, and doesn't even know the relationship between rough housing and boundary enforcement, and these aspects of the child, positive child development, like empathy and the difference between assertiveness and aggressiveness.

Gary: Dr. Ferrell, as we get to the top of the hour before we get there too quickly, I want people to first hear where they can find you and get ahold of your book.

Warren Farrell: Yes. The book is The Boy Crisis, and you can check that, just Google The Boy Crisis and Warren Farrell, Warren is W-A-R-R-E-N, and Farrell is F as in Frank, A-R-R-E-L-L. I used to not have to spell that but now people look up Will Ferrell with an E. So it's F-A-R-R-E-L-L. That's probably the easiest way to get ahold of that. If you want to take a deeper look at that, take a look at the website for warrenfarrell.com or The Boy Crisis.

Gary: Yeah, I'm going to get ahold of the book to read it, in thorough. I was reading excerpts off the website and some other things I found, because at some point, Doctor, I want to get you back on here so we can really talk a little further about the book other aspects of this, because it is a major problem in our society today that has to be dealt with. But I appreciate you taking the time to join me this morning.

Warren Farrell: And I appreciate the questions you asked and I appreciate your willingness to go deeply into it rather than just superficially into it.

Gary: Thank you, Dr. Farrell. Have a great weekend.

22

DR. PAUL KENGOR

Gary: Joining us now is Dr. Paul Kengor. Dr. Kengor is the New York Times best-selling author of A Pope and a President, God and Ronald Reagan, The Crusader and other books. Dr. Kengor is a doctor of political science and an executive director of the Center for Vision and Values at Grove City College. Good morning Doctor and welcome to the show.

Dr. Kengor: Hi, Gary! Good to be with you! Thanks.

Gary: So, we're going to talk about one of our native friends here. I don't know if we want to call him a friend, and here in Massachusetts, John Kerry. I read part of your book. I read part of the stuff that you've written about John. I've read some of your other books. But I've always found him just a bit too stiff for me, and an air about him that I don't like, and a lot of people around here, I'm not saying the majority, but a lot of people will agree. He's a very, very unique individual. Doctor, when you look up John Kerry and you do a chronology of his life, there's not enough paper to print it. I think he choreographed if he sneezed at Yale University.

Dr. Kengor: I think that's probably right. But again, stiff, that's the way a lot of people see him. And if you ever seen him in person, which you probably have.

Gary: I have.

Dr. Kengor: Yeah, yeah. A lot of people outside of your native area probably have not actually seen him in person. But, yeah. He does come across as literally stiff. Right? But he's been, boy, almost a household name in America for almost 50 years. In fact, to put an exact number on it, about 47 years, and I would take that back to the date April 22, 1971, when he gave his famous or infamous testimony to the Senate Foreign Relations Committee, and that had to do with the alleged war crimes committed by large groups in Vietnam and that made him an overnight sensation. It made him an overnight hero to some people, and make him an overnight villain to others. And that of course is the testimony where he infamously said that our troops, or soldiers in Vietnam, and this is the exact quote, "They committed war crimes, not isolated incidents, but crimes committed on a day-to-day basis with the full awareness of officers at all levels of command."

Think about those words, Gary. Right? Day-to-day basis. War crimes. Full awareness of officers at all levels of command. There's got to be some hyperbole.

Gary: Right.

Dr. Kengor: There's got to be. And then he said that US soldiers had quote, "Personally raped, cut off ears, cut off heads. Taped wires from portable telephones to human genitals and turned up the power." And this sounds like what happened with Iraqi soldiers to Kuwaiti citizens 1990. Cut off limbs, blown up bodies, randomly shot at civilians, raised villages in fashion reminiscent of Genghis Khan. He said, "Jen-jus Khan" is how he pronounced it in the audio. Shot cattle and dogs for fun. Poisoned food stocks and generally ravaged the country side of south Vietnam.

And again, even if some of that happened, he claimed in his testimony that this kind of stuff happened on a day-to-day basis with full awareness of officers at all levels of command. And that became the center room was packed with reporters. It was about a two-hour long testimony, and the next day, if not that day, the young John Kerry, not far from being a senator yet, was being discussed not only at CBS and ABC and NBC, but literally in the next white house, and probably also in Hinoi and probably also no exaggeration in the Kremlin as well.

Gary: When you listen to that testimony and then you read about John Kerry, I don't want to make light of it, but it was at the start of fake news, because when he was in Yale and he went into the service, there's a guy that used to go out on PT boats and video what he was doing, so he would have that information later on for whatever. Which is a little disturbing to me, Doctor.

Dr. Kengor: Right. Right.

Gary: Because, it was like he knew what he was going to do, and what he wanted to do, but when you listen to that testimony and then he failed to say any of the horrific things the Vietnamese were doing to American soldiers, we're at war, whether we agreed with that war, or we disagreed with the war. War is war. It's dirty, it's horrible, and with the more I read that testimony that you just brought up again, and I read it in detail, knowing that you were coming on the show again, boy, it doesn't sit well with me at all, but he was trying to define his future. That's the way I looked at it. He was trying to make his place to move forward. That what it amounted, and that's what he seems to have done his whole life.

Dr. Kengor: Yeah. Well, it's quite true, Gary, and there's no less a shrewd political observer than President Richard Nixon, who no matter what people thought of Nixon, the guy was a very shrewd politician. Bill Safire of the New York Times used to write all the time, right before every election, he would call up his old boss at the white house because Safire was a speech writer for Richard Nixon and he would get his prediction on the upcoming midterms or presidential election. Nixon just had this uncanny ability to be able to set aside whatever partisan belief that he had and really assess situations really well.

In fact, one of the reasons that Eisenhower picked Nixon as his running mate in 1952 was he already saw how good Nixon was as his political acumen. His ability to objectively look at situations. But my point of raising that, Nixon, right away saw Kerry as somebody with political ambition. And even dismissed him as a phony, and we have that on the Nixon tapes from the white house and he was talking to I think Haldeman and Ehrlichman, I can't remember which on exactly that it was. But he admitted that Kerry's testimony was really compelling and this is classic Nixon. He differentiated Kerry from the other, quote, "Bearded weirdos."

Gary: That's Nixon.

Dr. Kengor: As Nixon put it. Right? Referring to the Vietnam War protestors. Even though Kerry looked like a 70's dude, right?

Gary: Right.

Dr. Kengor: At testimony, his hair was a little bit long. And if you look at some of his Google photos of John Kerry and James together at the Vietnam war protests in the early 70's it's really weird to see that stuff. But, it was clear from the beginning that he was angling for some sort of political lot. And another native son of your area who got that was Edward Kennedy. Ed Kennedy, and it was senator Kennedy who at that point, I don't know 1971, couldn't have been in the senate for more than a half dozen years or so, and would've had to have been acquitted, two or three years.

Gary: Right.

Dr. Kengor: After that, but it was senator Kennedy who helped arrange for that Kerry testimony before the Senate Foreign Relations Committee, which by the way was done courtesy of senator William Fulbright, who was a mentor to Bill Clinton, which is one of those Clinton connections on civil rights, that liberals ought to be offended by, but look the other way, right?

Gary: Right.

Dr. Kengor: But Kennedy helped broker that for Kerry because I think Kennedy was also helping to groom Kerry to maybe run for congress or whatever and one day, not too far off in the future the two senators from Massachusetts, you'd have the senior senator Ted Kennedy and the junior senator John Kerry.

So, Kennedy, Fulbright, Nixon, and Kerry himself, they all had a pretty accurate sense of Kerry's political potential. And then of all things, he ended up getting the democratic nomination for president 2004, which was probably ultimately doomed by exactly what we're talking about here right now is his 1971 testimony against Vietnam vets.

Gary: Doctor, we're going to take a short break, but when we're trying to want to talk to you about some of his interference in the Trump white house.

Dr. Kengor: Right.

Gary:	You're listening to Business Politics and Lifestyles. My name is Gary Goldman, we'll be right back.

Gary: You're listening to Business Politics and Lifestyles. My name is Gary Goldman, we'll be right back.

On the phone with us now is Dr. Paul Kengor and we're speaking about John Kerry. Doctor, to me one of the best things Barack Obama did was appoint him to Secretary of State to get him out of the senate, so I wouldn't even have to look at his name on the ballad again. But that's just a personal little fetish of mine.

Dr. Kengor: That's probably the only way to get him out of the senate, wasn't it?

Gary: I think that was the only way to get out of the senate. When you talk about his testimony there and then you look at some of his actions as Secretary of State, and look back at the testimony about Vietnam, you could argue that this man has a distaste for America in a number of different avenues, and it came out in that hearing and it came out to me when he was Secretary of State.

Dr. Kengor: Well, and then of all things, after he was Secretary of State, and he's out of office, and what he considers one of the highlights of his time as Secretary of State was the Iran nuclear deal, many of which would consider a pretty dubious achievement, but he seems to think that it was a great thing, and Barack Obama does as well. Donald Trump made one of the things that he ran against and one of the quickest things that Trump did once he became president was try to cancel the deal. And did succeed in canceling the deal. Kind of confusing as to what the president can and can't do, exactly-

Gary: Right.

Dr. Kengor: How this works. So, Kerry was so worried and concerned that Trump was going to follow through on that, that it turns out that he actually met in New York, what were basically private meetings. In fact, the Boston Globe wrote the story. Credit to the Boston Globe. They describe it as a rare move of unusual shadowed diplomacy, they call it. It probably be seen a lot worse if it was done by someone in the Trump administration, but he met with the Iranian foreign minister, and other high level foreign officials from the Iranian government and as the Globe put it, I have the article right her. He managed to quote, and he did this while Trump was president and while Kerry was no longer Secretary of State. That's the key thing. He did this, quote, "to discuss ways of preserving the pact limiting Iran's nuclear weapons program".

And it was the second time in about two months that the two met to strategize over salvaging the deal, they spent years negotiating during the Obama administration. That's what the Globe reported. And some people listening who like Kerry and like Obama and like the Irani deal might say, "Great!" All right? But just think about this. I know it's your guy and your team and everything, but Kerry's no longer Secretary of State, and he's meeting privately like that while the current Secretary of State, the current state department, the current president which was duly elected, they're pursuing a different course.

And a lot of people right away raised the possibility that Kerry's actions might constitute a violation of the Logan Act, which frankly, it probably did. And then once you say that to Liberals, they say, "Well, no one's been persecuted under the Logan Act in over 200 years." Okay, all right, but-

Gary: Doesn't mean that we side step it.

Dr. Kengor: Right. That's exactly right. If that's the case, then do something to repudiate the Logan Act. I'm sure you'd be bringing it up if you could, if this was being done by a former republican Secretary of State against Barack Obama or against president Hilary Clinton.

So, what he was doing there was at the least probably unethical. Or it goes against the norms and quite possibly illegal and some people said, "treason". I don't like to use a word like that. That's a really, really high standard.

Gary: Right.

Dr. Kengor: Got to be tried in court and everything else and I'm not saying that. But it was at least objectionable and should raise some eyebrows.

Gary: Yeah, and I was surprised when I did see that article in the Boston Globe. Typical media just fluffed this off, Doctor. Like, "All right, it was just John Kerry being John Kerry as he likes to say, 'reporting for duty'." Someone need to tell him that duty had been called and he was out of office, but that's a whole other issue. But when I hear like the other day, rumblings. It's interesting, today, he's in Boston discussing, is it his new book? With the former governor of Massachusetts? Deval Patrick. I don't know. I read this in a lightning storm in the rain and listened to those two talk, but that not-

Dr. Kengor: I didn't even know that they had done that. So, they'd written a book together?

Gary: No, I think it's Kerry's book, but he's discussing it with Deval, the former governor.

Dr. Kengor: So, Kerry's talking about himself?

Gary: Talking about what he likes to do. To himself, he figured he'd bring someone in this time instead of doing it in a room by himself. But-

Dr. Kengor: Bring someone else to talk to-

Gary: Yeah, that will listen to his talk. But when you listen to him saying he hasn't ruled out a run for the presidency, that's when I know he's totally delusional.

Dr. Kengor: Yeah.

Gary: To think that really. If he couldn't do it last time, he's surely not going to do it again.

Dr. Kengor: Right, right. Well, and the talk at least outside of Massachusetts, I don't know how much there, where you guys are, but is that Elizabeth Warren would be the more likely person to run for president for Massachusetts.

Gary: Yeah, I think Elizabeth Warren could run for president. I think she'd be another great topic one day of conversation, because I think she's very dangerous, even based on some of the things she came out and said the other day about the president.

We do have a caller on the line that wants to speak to you. Joanne, good morning, welcome to the show.

Joanne: Hi! You know when you're talking about John Kerry. For me, it's like waving the red flag in front of a boat. Doctor, what about the swift boat guys that came forward and did undermine his campaign, thank God in their book, unfit for Command, that they wrote. Testimony after testimony by retired real admirals on down to the guys he served with on the Maycon Delta saying he was a poser, I lier, and none of this stuff was true that he said about the-

Gary: Vietnamese, yeah.

Joanne: And that was less than four months, because he wrote himself up for those other fake medals he gave himself. Unbelievable.

Dr. Kengor: Yeah, well, I'm glad you called. Very important.

Gary: Thanks Joanne.

Dr. Kengor: Yeah, and 2004, it really cost him in 2004 was not just that testimony from 1971, but you're right, how the swift boat veterans came out.

Gary: Right.

Dr. Kengor: And in fact that was led by John O'Neill and O'Neill went all the way back to the time that he and Kerry were on the Dick Cavett show. Now there's a blast from the past, right? Anybody over 50-

Gary: Yeah.

Dr. Kengor: Over 60 maybe at this point. But O'Neill was a guy who had taken command of Kerry's swift boat. And so he knew what happened. Very close. He was very close in time, physical proximity to it and he brought together that group. It was called Swift Boat Veterans for Truth. And to give you an idea of just how powerful that was, I think you guys will appreciate this, especially as I'm talking about age differences. I pulled up one of the courses I teach at Grove City College at Grove City Pennsylvania where I'm a professor, my students who are 18, 19, 20 years old, I pulled up that ad last

spring, because John Kerry was in the news and we were talking about political ads, and these kids were all three years old when that ad came out

Gary: Right.

Dr. Kengor: None of them had seen it before. Their jaws, Gary, hit the table, and one of them just gasped and said to me, "That is incredible!" And they panned through all those different guys who were all in their 60's at that point. They showed all their faces. John Kerry lied, John Kerry deceived his country, and you could just see. The one student said, "That is devastating!"

Gary: Right.

Dr. Kengor: I said, "Well, you're right and that's the effect that it had in 2004." You want to know who beat John Kerry in 2004? Might have been less George W. Bush then John O'Neill in the Swift Boat Veterans Committee.

Gary: We have another caller. John on the line. Got less than a minute, John how are you?

John: I'm fine, thank you. I just wanted to say I'm so happy to hear, Doctor Kengor. My son had him as a professor at Grove City College, and he would bring home all his text books for me to read-

Gary: Right.

John: Because he thought the professor was outstanding. And I especially read and was frightened by the book about Obama's mentor, I think the book was called The Communist. But anyway, thanks for being on, Doctor Kengor.

| **Gary:** | Yup. |

| John: | It was great to hear your voice. |

| **Gary:** | John, thank you for the call. Doctor, we're at the top of the hour. How can people quickly get a hold of you? |

| Dr. Kengor: | Yeah, well, I guess my books are at Amazon.com. Just type in Paul Kengor. Check out our website for the Center for Vision and Value. |

| **Gary:** | Thank you, Doctor, it was great speaking with you this morning. |

| Dr. Kengor: | All right. Thanks, Gary. |

| **Gary:** | Have a great morning. |

23

BERNARD KERIK

Gary: On the line with me now is Bernard Kerik. Mr. Kerik just released his first fiction novel, The Grave Above the Grave. Mr. Kerik served as the 40th police commissioner of New York City; prior to his appointment he was a commission of the Department of Correction, a recipient of the prestigious New York Police Department Medal of Valor. Mr. Kerik is the author of a New York Times best-selling memoir of The Lost Son, A Life in Pursuit of Justice, a law enforcement insider and frequent media commentator.

Mr. Kerik welcome to the show, nice speaking with you again.

Bernard Kerik: Thank you, sir.

Gary: So I want to talk about the book The Grave Above the Grave. First of all, what prompted you to go write this book? You can tell our listeners a little bit about the book as well.

Bernard Kerik: Well listen as you said, I had a New York Times best seller, The Lost Son, I'd written another bio following that, and based on my time in the NYPD, my time in counter terrorism measures and also I actually lived in Saudi Arabia for four years, I've worked for the King of Jordan for close to five years, so I have a pretty good understanding, better than normal of the enemies who we face in this country. And I threw that into the context of a novel, and it's basically about a fictional New York City police commissioner, imagine, and he gets involved in a present day terrorism investigation, but he has reflections dating back to 9/11 because he was the precinct commander in the precinct where the towers were and his wife was killed on one of the planes.

So it makes for a compelling read and it also educates the reader as to what my mindset is on what the threats we face in the future are, how these people operate, how they train, how they plan, how they communicate, how they get into the country. And I think people will find it interesting.

Gary: Yeah, that's the part. I mean if there was a take away that's the take away that I received is reading it I'm thinking, "Well this has to be where he thinks we are in regard to terrorism, where things are going, and the things that we should be concerned about." Do you think we've become a little too complacent in this country thinking it can't happen again, or do you think we really are on high alert and high guard?

Bernard Kerik: I think we get complacent. The unfortunate thing is things like September 11th they motivate people, they unite people, they inspire people to get out and do what they're supposed, but I have to tell you living through it and having been through a number of other crises like this, after 90, maybe 120 days, that interest, that unity, that concern starts to diminish. Right now, today in Congress you have members of the United States Congress that are not supporting medical programs for first responders that are basically dying. There's 10,000 of them that have these toxic cancer related issues in New York City and we have members of Congress that they're saying they're not going to support the bills to get them the funding they need to take care of themselves.

But within 60 to 90 days after September 11th I promise you they would have signed anything.

Gary: Right, right, and you know you're so right, 'cause after that cycle goes through and the kumbaya seems to end, it's got to at some point make the investigative process at times a little difficult, because when people are alert and they're more aware they're probably helpful. I'm at least assuming they may be helpful in investigating certain things, now they sort of say, "Yeah well, let's see where things go."

Bernard Kerik: No you're absolutely right, and it also hurts, it diminishes the interest on the outside, so when you have incidents like San Francisco, Orlando, Boston, every one of those scenarios you had neighbors and friends and people, associates with them, colleagues that basically said, "I knew it. I knew there was something wrong. I knew I should have called. I saw something." Whatever, but they didn't. And that's because the interest, the concern has been diminished over time.

Gary: Yeah, and I think the reality is people right away, if they bring something up, they can be... The name calling, the labeling, "You're a racist." It's not just telling someone you're doing this because there's some other motive on your behalf, and that stops people from moving forward at times too, Mr. Kerik.

Bernard Kerik: You're absolutely right.

Gary: Which is horrible. And when you look at these terrorist events, people were thinking something would happen right away, but having studied some of this, these guys plan this stuff out. The next worst event may not be a year, it may be five years, ten years, but to me they're always planning their next horrific event.

Bernard Kerik: That's right, and that's a really good point. Osama Bin Laden used to tell all of his followers when you do something you want a spectacular event; you want something spectacular, and 9/11 for sure was spectacular in many different ways. The bottom line is today you don't need another 9/11, you don't need four planes flying into buildings. You can have five two man teams go into five cities on Monday afternoon, all over this country, walk into elementary schools and execute a bunch of kids. I promise you, it's going to be spectacular. So the importance of our intelligence capabilities working, the importance of planning and preparation and being on top of this stuff is extremely important. It's extremely important because these guys never go away. They'll wait you out. We have no patience, they have plenty.

Gary: Yeah, it is amazing how they will wait you out. And it brings me to mind, because one event that occurred in this country, the shooting in Las Vegas, people feel they haven't been told the truth or the real answer, when they hear that a lot of times officials would say, "We're really not sure." Or they'd give you some haphazard situation that may have occurred. I don't know, I personally think we haven't been told exactly what happened there.

Bernard Kerik: Well, sometimes you get the whole scoop, sometimes you get some, and sometimes you get misinformation. The bottom line, on the authorities side, there's some stuff they can't tell you-

Gary: Right.

Bernard Kerik: And one thing that your listeners may be interested in is we have thwarted probably 70 or 80 attacks over the last 17 years since 9/11. Many of those your listeners wouldn't even have heard of, nobody even knows about. So there's this constant push to get the job done and make sure people are safe. Sometimes you get, sometimes you don't.

Gary:

You know and law enforcement and investigators, you've been in that role, have to be frustrated when you see a situation like this. I think it was down in New Mexico where they broke up that group of individuals that were training children to go into schools, and then because of a technicality a lot of these people are allowed to walk, which to me, Joe, ordinary citizen, it's absurd. And the second part of that is, it's going to cost the government that much more now to follow these people or it becomes another obstacle. And I think the frustration on law enforcement and even sometimes prosecutors to what's going is it's sometimes the laws don't seem in rhythm with reality.

Bernard Kerik:

No, you could not be more right, especially in today's political environment in Washington. You know that thing in New Mexico was outrageous. And basically they had to release them because the state prosecutor didn't follow up and produce the things they had to produce before the court. And the judge was mandated, had no choice but to let them go. Luckily the Federal Government came in and they have now brought charges. Where that's going to go I don't know, but I think there has to be a focus on our entire criminal justice system. People are putting people in prison for you know, commercial fisherman for catching too many fish, and yet they're not following up on things where they're training young people to go into schools and kill people. It's nuts.

Gary:

Yeah, and speaking of, and I do want to, before I let you go, touch base on the criminal justice system, there is something very wrong, because you look at individuals that should be locked up after being arrested that are allowed to walk, it's some of the simplest, not the simplest, not the right word, but a crime that's committed that should be dealt with differently. They're put in prison, they're really not hardened criminals, and you and I have talked about this in the past, and when they leave prison they're hardened, now they are hardened criminals and their lives are ruined, they've been labeled, they can't get a job. There's something very wrong, but what frustrates me Mr. Kerik, nobody wants to touch this. They claim they're touching it, but they don't want to deal with it.

Bernard Kerik: Well listen, members of Congress don't want to deal with it, because they're afraid that they're going to be looked at like they're not being tough on crime. Problem is you have to smart on crime. You've got to be in a position where bad people that do bad things go to prison. People that you're afraid of go to prison. People that you're mad at, they do stupid things, they don't need prison. First time non-violent offenders don't need prison. Sure they'll get the message just by the conviction alone, because the conviction in itself is a lifelong punishment of collateral consequence. It destroys you personally, financially, and professionally. I mean, how much more do you want to punish a guy?

Now if it's a murderer or a rapist or a robbery suspect or somebody with gun charges, those guys need to be held. Those guys need to be in prison, keep them off the streets, I get it. But the system is definitely flawed.

Gary: Yeah, even when you look at some of the white-collar crime, and again, you commit a crime there should be a price. I say put these people out talking and educating people to make them aware of-

Bernard Kerik: You're one hundred percent right.

Gary: It's insane. Locking them in a prison and not doing anything to get the message out is absolutely absurd. It's frustrating and I've read a lot of stuff that you've had to say about this and I couldn't agree with you more and I think we have to remain focused on this because here in lovely Massachusetts we seem to let more of the bad guys out, and it's either for some crazy reason or the prisons are too full or whatever the case may be. But then you study the cases, the individuals that are in there, they shouldn't be there, make the room for the guys that you're talking about, or girls.

Bernard Kerik: You're right, you're absolutely right.

Gary: So how can people find your book? Get a hold of you etc.?

Bernard Kerik: Listen the book is on amazon.com, Barnes and Noble, all your primary bookstores. I think you'd find it a compelling read, I think it'd be educational. If you like cops, terrorism, and all that stuff you see in the movies, this is the book.

Gary: No, it's a great book and like I said, having read it, exactly what you said, my impression is these are things that as the commissioner or going forward you have seen that we should be aware of. Mr. Kerik I appreciate you joining me this morning. I look forward to talking with you again shortly, and have a wonderful rest of the weekend.

Bernard Kerik: Thank you sir.

24

DR. TIM BALL

Gary: This morning we are joined by climate change analyst Dr. Tim Ball. Dr. Ball is the author of Human Caused Global Warming; The Biggest Deception in History. Dr. Ball is an environmental consultant and former climatologist professor at the University of Winnipeg in Manitoba.

Dr. Ball good morning and welcome to the show.

Dr. Tim Ball: Good morning Gary and thanks for the opportunity.

Gary: It's great having you here. So again this week a hurricane along the East Coast of the United States. They were right, this is going to be the worst storm in history. You know, not to downplay the effects of a hurricane because anyone who is affected by it, it doesn't matter, but this is gonna be the worst storm, another result of global warming and this is churning along the Carolina coast and slows down. When it gets there it sort of goes from four to one, which is still a devastating storm. The constant wanting to tie a hurricane up here in New England, whether it's a winter storm, into part of a global climate change they just won't stop, that rhetoric won't stop Doctor.

Dr. Tim Ball: No it won't. And to give you an example, they persisted in saying that the winds were 75 miles an hour. The reason that they did that is because if it goes to 74 than in their system it is no longer a hurricane. Of course, they are the ones that measure and determine, they, meaning NOAH, the National Oceanographic and Atmospheric Administration, they are the ones that determine what the wind speeds are. One of the things that happened with this was, as with Katrina by the way, and as with all the hurricanes, they are unable to determine the wind speed at the base of the hurricane. So what they do is they fly through at high altitude, and they take the wind speed up there and using a computer model estimate what the wind speed is at the surface.

In every single case so far since they've been using this method it gives higher readings than actually are occurring, which they can determine, of course, once the hurricane gets on shore. And as I said, the hurricane category is determined by the wind speed. And you saw it with Katrina, they were absolutely determined between both the weather office, and the media to have it as a category five, and Katrina briefly, an hour maybe, they claimed it was a category five, but when it got ashore it barely made a three. Now as you said, "Was there flooding? Was there damage? Was there loss of life?" But what you see as you look at hurricanes through time, the biggest loss of life is because the government creates an illusion of safety. The first example of this, the big example, was in 1900 when the hurricane hit Galveston Texas, and the government built a wall to protect against the surge, and it just simply blew right through that and 12,000 people drowned.

And the same was true of Katrina. The U.S. Army Corp of Engineers wanted to improve the dyke that was protecting New Orleans and particularly the poor low lying area, and the environmentalists blocked them from doing it and guess what happened? And why are the weather offices involved in this?

This is the biggest bureaucratic deep state fake news story, as I said the global warming is the biggest deception in history. The whole idea that human CO2 is causing global warming was created through the United Nations through an organization called the Inter-Governmental Panel on Climate Change. It was set up through the World Meteorological Organization, which is made up of the weather experts in every national weather office in every member country of the United Nations. So the bureaucrats are the ones that created this whole thing through the U.N., and they're the ones of course who are pushing it. This was done deliberately.

Mars Strong, the guy that orchestrated all this, new that if he could control the bureaucrats he could control the politicians. The politicians don't know enough to question it and if they do they're quickly put down, just the way that people like me, that dared to stand up and say, "Hey your science is wrong." Oh, he's paid by the oil companies or, as in my case with three lawsuits that have cost me $600,000 in legal bills so far. So this is just the biggest fake news story in history, and the worst deep state perpetuated issue. Think about what they spent, trillions on climate change, trillions, and think of what they could've done, things that need to be dealt with.

Gary: Yeah and that's usually the case. What's incredible is they dislike President Trump. I'm reading articles this week already, President Trump's new environmental policies, he's to blame for this, which we both know is absolutely absurd. It's just another way to shut what the truth is.

But what they really don't like, Doctor, is that when he sees a hurricane coming, the preparedness that he does, the things he does in advance that a lot of other administrations doesn't do sort of takes a lot of thunder out of their arguments in a lot of cases because when you prepare, it's an environment, it's the weather, but when you're prepared for and there's not the "disaster" going on afterwards. When you minimize that it takes their thunder away.

Dr. Tim Ball: No, definitely. And of course this is the whole problem with Trump. That all of the professional politicians, because that's all we have now in the swamp. I've even heard Mitch McConnel say he's not capable of being a president. Well, how dare he say that but that's what these political people think, left and right. So here he comes along, and he does a better job than any of them, how much is that in your face? Of course, if they hate him to start off with when he can come along do a better job than they can do, it just underscores what failures they are and have been. So, yeah, this is very part of it.

By the way, disclaimer here, I was summoned to Washington to be part of a team that was going to advise President Trump on what to do about the EPA which was the bureaucracy used to push all these regulations that are controlling people's lives, and also what to do about the global warming issue. We advised him not to argue against the global warming issue on the basis of bad science, although it is terrible science, but to do it on the basis that the Paris Climate Accord is a bad deal.

Dr. Tim Ball: This is what they're now blaming him for, for getting out of the Paris Climate Accord and saying, "Without that this hurricane wouldn't have occurred, wouldn't have been so bad." But the reality was the Paris Climate Accord was a bad deal and we had proof of that because we were told when we said to him "get of the Paris Climate deal", we got word back that Ivanka wanted him to sign it.

We said just show Ivanka, she's a business woman, show her the deal. She looked at the deal and of course said, "Yeah no problem." By the way, most of the other countries that are accusing the U.S. and Trump are not meeting the requirements for the Paris Climate Accord. They're not putting the money in and yet the countries that are supposed to get money from the deal are saying, "We want our cash!" Here's the reality of it Gary, even if the Paris Climate agreement was totally implemented, that is every country reduced its CO2 by the amount that they agreed to reduce it, if all of them did that, by the year 2030 that would result in a reduction of temperature of .086 degrees Fahrenheit by 2100. That's how ridiculous this is.

So even if they did what they said they're going to do the effects... that reduction, by the way, of .086, less than 1 degree Fahrenheit, that's within the error of estimate of their data.

Gary: Exactly

Dr. Tim Ball: So even if they did it, it wouldn't have made any difference-

Gary: Dr. Ball we are going to take a quick break and when we come back I want to talk about the delusional theories these people have as well as the cyclical part of the weather they don't understand.

On the line with us now is climate change analyst Dr. Tim Ball.

Dr. Ball, it's amazing if you go back and look at weather cycles you'll see some of the things they claim, that major storms are very large hurricanes or winter storms. You go back in time you can almost follow patterns of these types of storms.

Dr. Tim Ball: Exactly and this is what got me into this whole area of climate and I've been doing it for 40 years. But the first nine years the weather I had to deal with went with flying. I was in the Canadian Air Force flying anti-submarine patrols over the North Atlantic chasing Russian submarines around. No one ever told us what to do if we caught one. But anyway, the other thing was that I spent five years of search and rescue flying in arctic Canada. After nine years of this, and also, by the way, teaching my fellow students on how to read the weather forecast. I lost my flying category because of hearing loss, and so I decided to go back to university and try and find out why the weather forecasting was so bad.

It hasn't improved very much in 150 years, by the way. They still, once you get beyond 72 hours, are very very inaccurate. You look at what they did with hurricane Florence they had nine computer models giving a different forecast, each of them gave a different track for the hurricane. None of them were correct and that's in a small area where supposedly they've got a lot of data.

What I did was, to get to your question, I started to look at, well why is forecasting so bad. I discovered that a Hubert Lamb in England who had been doing forecasting during the war for pilots flying over Germany. They were complaining about the bad forecast so Lamb started to look at it as well. I spent quite a lot of time with him and what we did was we started reconstructing past weather patterns which you were talking about, and we see that the weather in the path has been very very dramatically different, the climate changes all the time, and it changes far more than people understand.

Just to give you one example, if we take the last 10,000 years of global temperature and we get this from ice cores in Greenland and Antarctica, the last 10,000 years of the Earth's temperature it has been warmer for 97% of that 10,000 years than it is today. Yet, they are telling you that today is as warm as it's ever been. This is an absolute lie. Now, one of the problems is that you and I are talking about cycles. There are people in the stock market, as you know, that follow weather cycles and use them for-

Gary:	Commodities, yeah.

Dr. Tim Ball:	Yeah exactly. The commodities and so on. The Russians were the first to start doing that. There is a thing called the Cape Cycle the Kondratieff Cycle which is based upon grain harvest based upon the drought cycles in the middle latitudes. That's been around for over 100 years. The Russians and the Chinese, and I've worked with both of them, they both have very long-term records of weather and crop production, and they argue that there are cycles in this. But the Western world, America and Europe, they don't believe there are cycles. They believe that the weather is chaotic. At a conference in 1991 in Warsaw, this came to a battle and the media reported it, of course, as a cold war battle of ideology when in fact it was actually a scientific battle over the patterns of weather.

Dr. Tim Ball:	I teased the western people saying, "You better hope that it's chaotic and can't be forecasted because that will give you an excuse about why your forecasts are so bad." That's precisely what we are looking at. Yes, if you look at long term weather patterns, and I don't mean just the 30 years or even the-

Gary:	No, No

Dr. Tim Ball:	Even the hundred years of official weather patterns. That's not long enough to understand the cycles of weather. Weather cycles are much much longer than that.

Gary:	Because nowadays the media gets involved and in people's mind, they think a cycle is 10, 20, 30 years and that is just not the case. Somehow, we do need to take the hostility and emotion out of this talk about climate change, just to make sure that we're doing things and preserving things that we should be, but Doctor I don't see that happening.

Gary:　　If you disagree with someone who believes in all of this the conversation just ends. They do not want to have a normal conversation and talk about it with you.

Dr. Tim Ball:　　Exactly. It's absolutely remarkable that people who know virtually nothing about it have such definitive positions on it. As you said, even if you present them with a few facts they will reject it either by saying "well I just don't want to hear that" or by, as I said, personal attacks on you ad hominem attacks "oh you're paid by the oil companies" or some other thing. By the way, it's very interesting the oil companies are being attacked because they produce the CO_2 that they're blaming for global warming. The reality is that this is where the fundamental problem is, that all of the records we have, going back thousands of years, shows that the temperature changes before the CO_2. In other words, the basic assumption they make that the CO_2 increase causes the temperature increase-

Gary:　　Is wrong.

Dr. Tim Ball:　　Is absolutely wrong. There's no evidence of that whatsoever. In fact, what the long-term records show, and even the short-term records, show that the temperature changes before the CO_2. The only place in the world where a CO_2 increase causes a temperature increase is in the computer models that they created and wrote the code for.

Of course, that explains why, and this is the most damning thing of all, every single forecast that the IPCC have made since 1990, every single one has been wrong. Yet, they continue to say that they know what they're doing and their science is correct. The simple fact is that if your prediction is wrong your science is wrong. End of story. But this is the degree of manipulation that goes on.

After 1998 and yes prior to 1998 CO2 was going up and the temperature was going up. It appeared that their theory was correct. But after 1992 the CO2 continued to rise but the temperature started to level off. By 2004 it was already causing a PR problem because if you think back to Boston and what was going on with snow and cold winters and people it became a joke. They said, "Well why are we having all this cold and snowy weather?" And they said, "Oh it's due to global warming." That started to raise people's eyebrows right there. There were emails that were leaked from the science people at the University of East Anglia that were producing all of this false science. The emails that were leaked in 2004 from the guy or the center that was responsible for PR, it said, "Look I'm having a hard time with the media asking questions about the fact that your theory doesn't fit the reality anymore and maybe we should stop calling it global warming and start calling it climate change".

The Swedish climate representative on IPCC sends an email back saying, "Yeah that's a good idea". And that's precisely what they did-

Gary: That's what changed.

Dr. Tim Ball: When their forecasts were wrong, their predictions were wrong, they didn't go back and say "well our science is wrong", they moved the goalpost-

Gary: Yeah, you know-

Dr. Tim Ball: They stopped calling it global warming and started calling it climate change. This is why I say it's the biggest deception in history.

Gary: Doctor when I watch one of these hurricane forecasts, theoretically I said, "If they want to manipulate the forecast, the hurricane could be heading for Hawaii and they'd make the computer model still bring it to the Carolinas". I just don't have a lot of faith in them anymore.

Gary: As we get to the bottom of the hour, how can people get a hold of you or get a hold of your book?

Dr. Tim Ball: They can get a hold of my book through Amazon.com or if they go to my website drtimball.com, that's d-r-t-i-m-b-a-l-l.com, and either one will take them to that. Through the website they can get a whole lot more information, all the articles, and materials that I published.

Gary: It's been great speaking with you this morning. As I like to tell my friends when they get into this argument, "You're entitled to your opinion but not your own facts".

Dr. Tim Ball: Exactly. Of course, facts don't mean anything in today's fake news world.

Gary: They don't. Dr. Ball thank you so much for joining me.

Dr. Tim Ball: Thank you for the opportunity Gary and thanks for what you're doing presenting both sides of an argument and letting people make up their own mind, which is what they don't want you to do.

Gary: Thank you and have a great day.